# Working Hard, Working Happy

In this new book from Routledge and MiddleWeb, author Rita Platt shows how you can create a joyful classroom community in which students are determined to work hard, be resilient, and never give up. She describes how to help build students' purpose, mastery, and autonomy, so they take ownership over their work and develop a growth mindset for success.

Topics covered include:

- Why joy and effort go hand in hand
- How to build a classroom climate of caring and achievement
- Why mastery and goal setting are important
- How to work with differentiated instruction
- How to work with cooperative and collaborative learning
- Why parent-teacher connection is vital
- How to take your practice of joy and effort beyond the classroom
- And much more!

Each chapter includes practical tools, tips, and ideas that you can use immediately to develop these skills in students, so they find more joy and success in the learning process.

**Rita Platt** (@ritaplatt) is a National Board Certified, award-winning teacher. She is a self-proclaimed #edudork with master's degrees in reading, library, and leadership. Her experience includes teaching learners from preschool through adult in remote Alaskan villages, inner cities, and rural communities. She is currently a school principal, teaches graduate courses for the Professional Development Institute and writes for MiddleWeb.

# Also Available from Routledge Eye On Education and MiddleWeb
www.routledge.com/collections/11190

**Write, Think, Learn:**
Tapping the Power of Daily Student Writing Across the Content Areas
Mary K. Tedrow

**Creating Citizens:**
Teaching Civics and Current Events in the History Classroom, 6–9
Sarah Cooper

**Close Reading the Media:**
Literacy Lessons and Activities for Every Month of the School Year
Frank W. Baker

**The Genius Hour Guidebook:**
Fostering Passion, Wonder, and Inquiry in the Classroom
Denise Krebs and Gallit Zvi

**STEM by Design:**
Strategies and Activities for Grades 4–8
Anne Jolly

**The Flexible ELA Classroom:**
Practical Tools for Differentiated Instruction in Grades 4–8
Amber Chandler

**History Class Revisited:**
Tools and Projects to Engage Middle School Students in Social Studies
Jody Passanisi

**Two Teachers in the Room:**
Strategies for Co-Teaching Success
Elizabeth Stein

**It's a Matter of Fact:**
Teaching Students Research Skills in Today's Information-Packed World
Angie Miller

# Working Hard, Working Happy

Cultivating a Culture of Effort and Joy in the Classroom

Rita Platt

NEW YORK AND LONDON

First published 2020
by Routledge
52 Vanderbilt Avenue, New York, NY 10017

and by Routledge
2 Park Square, Milton Park, Abingdon, Oxon, OX14 4RN

*Routledge is an imprint of the Taylor & Francis Group, an informa business*

© 2020 Taylor & Francis

The right of Rita Platt to be identified as author of this work has been asserted by her in accordance with sections 77 and 78 of the Copyright, Designs and Patents Act 1988.

All rights reserved. No part of this book may be reprinted or reproduced or utilised in any form or by any electronic, mechanical, or other means, now known or hereafter invented, including photocopying and recording, or in any information storage or retrieval system, without permission in writing from the publishers.

*Trademark notice*: Product or corporate names may be trademarks or registered trademarks, and are used only for identification and explanation without intent to infringe.

*Library of Congress Cataloging-in-Publication Data*
A catalog record for this book has been requested

ISBN: 978-0-367-25732-3 (hbk)
ISBN: 978-0-367-25733-0 (pbk)
ISBN: 978-0-429-28949-1 (ebk)

Typeset in Palatino
by Apex CoVantage, LLC

# Dedication

Writing a book is a huge undertaking. I am so grateful to all of the "families" in my life who made this book possible by supporting me, loving me, pushing me to do my best, and making me laugh just when I needed to. First and foremost, this book is dedicated to my husband, John Wolfe, my beautiful children, Kenneth and Azalea Miner, my good friend and the father of my children, Kevin Miner, my father, Steven Platt, my sister and best friend, Susie "Titi" Platt, and my brother-in-law Speedy Pete. Though it might sound silly, I also want to formally thank my fur-family, my dogs Honey Bee and Snoopy and my cats Callie (RIP), Sasha, and Shadow for the pets and purrs that kept me cool and calm while I worked. Second, big thank yous to my MiddleWeb family, John Croft Norton and Susan B. Curtis, you are the best of the best. I also want to thank my education family: Ken Swift, Trena Richardson, Kevin and Karlin Uhde, Vern and Irene Brenner, Alasha Woods, Ivy Burns, Jeff Benoy, Randi Shaw, Stacey Belisle, The PDI Team, and every educator, family, and student that I have ever worked with. Through you, I learned and continue to learn. Finally, and perhaps most importantly, I want to thank Lauren Davis who is without a doubt the kindest, most supportive editor and publisher in the world.

# Contents

| | | |
|---|---|---|
| **1** | **Working Hard, Working Happy** | 1 |
| | The Big Idea | 2 |
| | My Five-part Philosophy | 2 |
| | How to Read This Book | 7 |
| | | |
| **2** | **Joy and Effort, Best Friends Forever!** | 10 |
| | The Theory and Research | 10 |
| | Joy Matters! | 11 |
| |    Simple Tips, Hints, and Ideas to Increase Joy | 14 |
| |       1 Don't feel it? Fake it, until you make it by "acting as if . . . " | 15 |
| |       2 Laugh at your own jokes | 15 |
| |       3 Play music | 15 |
| |       4 YouTube it | 16 |
| |       5 Use games and technology | 16 |
| |       6 Practice gratitude | 17 |
| | Hard Work Matters Too! | 18 |
| |    What Rigor is, What Rigor is NOT | 19 |
| |    The GRR and Friends! | 20 |
| |    Motivation Theory | 23 |
| |    The Role of Self-control in Hardworking and Happy Classrooms | 24 |
| |    Simple Tips, Hints, and Ideas to Help you Build a Hardworking Classroom | 25 |
| |       1 Make learning targets clear | 26 |
| |       2 Do less but do it better | 27 |
| |       3 Breed success | 27 |
| |       4 Teach growth mindset | 28 |
| |       5 Brand your classroom | 28 |
| | Joy and Effort, BFFs! | 29 |
| | | |
| **3** | **Where Everyone Knows Your Name** | 31 |
| | What is School or Classroom Climate? | 32 |
| | The Theory and Research | 32 |
| |    It is All About Relationships | 32 |
| |    Simple Tips, Hints, and Ideas to Foster Positive Relationships | 35 |
| |       1 Have some low-key fun! | 35 |
| |       2 Flip the fun on Flipgrid! | 35 |

    *3 Conduct interest inventories*   36
    *4 Keep culture in mind*   37
  Building a Safe Climate of Caring and Achievement   38
   Safety in Routines and Management   39
    *Routines*   39
    *Management*   44
    *Starting with clear rules and consequences for not respecting them*   44
    *Consequences*   45
   Being Proactive   46
    *The four main functions of behavior*   47
   Simple Tips, Hints, and Ideas for Managing a Classroom   50
    *1 Use technology tools*   50
    *2 The character education connection*   51
    *3 Go visiting!*   51
    *4 Assume best intentions!*   52
   What if Your Classroom is "Out of Control"?   52

**4  Mastery Matters!**   **56**
  Mastery Matters   57
   The Theory and Research   57
   Big Wins!   58
   A Quest for Quality   60
    *What is quality?*   60
    *Inspiring quality*   61
    *Ideas for supporting quality written work*   61
   Focus on the Standards   63
   Simple Tips, Hints, and Ideas to Help Move Students to Mastery   66
    *1 Teach students positive self-talk and a growth mindset!*   66
    *2 Focus on the power of "yet!"*   67
  Goal Setting With Students   68
   A Step-by-step Plan for Teaching Goal Setting   68
   Simple Tips, Hints, and Ideas to Motivate Learners Through Goal setting   72
    *1 Celebrate!*   72
    *2 Keep families in the loop*   72
    *3 Use goal-setting forms*   73
    *4 Model by setting and sharing your own goals*   73
  Mastery Makes a Difference   74

**5  Have it Your Way! Differentiated Instruction**   **75**
  Ode on a Boring In-service   75
  What is Differentiated Instruction?   77

| | |
|---|---|
| The Theory and Research | 79 |
| Voice and Choice | 80 |
|     How Voice and Choice Impact Motivation | 80 |
|     Simple Tips, Hints, and Ideas to Allow for Voice and Choice | 80 |
|         1 *Surveying students* | 81 |
|         2 *Build choice into assignments* | 81 |
| Formative Assessment | 82 |
|     Simple Tips, Hints, and Ideas for Formative Assessment | 82 |
|         1 *Exit tickets* | 82 |
|         2 *3, 2, 1 Quick write* | 83 |
|         3 *Self-assessment* | 83 |
|         4 *Simple checklists* | 84 |
|         5 *Google forms* | 85 |
| Types of Differentiation | 86 |
|     Steps to Differentiation | 88 |
|     Simple Tips, Hints, and Ideas for Differentiation | 90 |
|         1 *Tic-Tac-Toe boards (differentiation by process and product)* | 91 |
|         2 *HyperDocs (differentiation by process and product)* | 93 |
|         3 *Tiered assignments (differentiation by content, process, and product)* | 93 |
|         4 *Flexible seating (differentiation by process and product)* | 95 |
| The Role of Reading in Differentiated Instruction | 99 |
|     Two Categories of Texts | 99 |
|     Simple Tips, Hints, and Ideas for Differentiated Instruction with Grade-level Texts | 100 |
|         1 *Don't just assign – teach* | 101 |
|         2 *Intentional partner reading* | 101 |
|         3 *Pre-teach vocabulary* | 101 |
|         4 *Teach SQ3R* | 101 |
|         5 *Use close reading* | 103 |
|     Simple Tips, Hints, and Ideas for Using Leveled Texts | 104 |
|         1 *Individualized and all together thematic reading (IATT)* | 104 |
|         2 *Resources for leveled (differentiated) texts* | 105 |
|     A Reminder: it's not an Either/or Thing | 106 |
| **6 Social Animals** | **108** |
| 21st-century Skills | 109 |
| Students Learning from Students | 111 |
|     Focusing the Message with Social Proof | 111 |
|     Simple Tips, Hints, and Ideas to Harness the Power of Social Proof | 112 |
|         1 *Big read, little read* | 112 |
|         2 *Look who's reading!* | 113 |

|   |   |
|---|---|
|     3 *Reading friends* | 113 |
|     4 *Writer's conference* | 113 |
|     5 *Virtual visits* | 114 |
| Cooperative and Collaborative Learning | 115 |
|     Collaborative and Cooperative Learning in Practice | 115 |
|     Simple Tips, Hints, and Ideas for Using Collaborative and Cooperative Learning | 116 |
|         1 *Cross-age tutoring* | 116 |
|         2 *Kagan strategies* | 117 |
|         3 *Collaborative worksheets, reviews, and lectures* | 119 |
|     Classroom Management – a Quick Review | 121 |
|     We Need Each Other! | 121 |

## 7 Busting Down the Walls, Building Community Connections — **124**

|   |   |
|---|---|
| Why Bother? | 125 |
| Involvement Versus Engagement of Caregivers | 126 |
| A Framework for Caregiver Engagement | 127 |
| Positive Phone Calls and Social Media Sharing | 128 |
|     Reach Out and Touch Someone! | 128 |
|     Social Media Sharing | 130 |
|     Simple Tips, Hints, and Ideas to Communicate with Caregivers | 131 |
|         1 *Be transparent!* | 132 |
|         2 *Judge less, love more* | 132 |
|         3 *Look approachable!* | 132 |
|         4 *Watch out for RBF and smile, smile, smile!* | 133 |
| Be Visible! | 133 |
|     Simple Tips, Hints, and Ideas to be Present in Your Students' Communities | 134 |
|         1 *More on meetups . . .* | 134 |
|         2 *Get your sports on!* | 135 |
|         3 *Home visits* | 135 |

## 8 Effort and Joy, They're Not Just for Students! — **137**

|   |   |
|---|---|
| Focus On Your Efforts Where They Matter! | 139 |
|     Define Your Values | 139 |
|     Using Your Values to Make Decisions | 142 |
|         *Examples from the field* | 142 |
|     Continued Learning | 144 |
|         *Graduate credit on the cheap* | 145 |
|         *Professional Development Institute (PDI)* | 145 |
|         *MOOCs (massive online open courses)* | 145 |
|         *Twitter* | 145 |

|  |  |
|---|---|
| *Edcamp* | 146 |
| *Google (Yes, I said, "Google!")* | 146 |
| Simple Tips, Hints, and Ideas for Focusing Your Efforts in the Classroom | 147 |
|    *1 Collaborate and communicate* | 147 |
|    *2 Stay in the power zone* | 147 |
|    *3 One sentence lesson plans* | 148 |
|    *4 Purge!* | 149 |
|    *5 Divide your to-do list* | 149 |
| Staying Joyful! | 150 |
|   Start and End With Love | 150 |
|   Stop the Ripples of Rudeness | 150 |
|   Practice Self-care | 152 |
|   Simple Tips, Hints, and Ideas to Keep You Joyful in the Classroom | 154 |
|    *1 Learn to say "No"!* | 154 |
|    *2 Don't obsess* | 154 |
|    *3 Recognize that great can be the enemy of good enough* | 154 |
|    *4 Get out there and have fun!* | 155 |
| **9 Conclusion** | **157** |
| Remember the BIG Idea | 157 |
| The Five-part Philosophy | 157 |
| Okay. Joy & Effort. Now What? | 158 |

# 1

# Working Hard, Working Happy

> **The BIG Idea**
> *Classrooms that develop a culture of joy and effort are classrooms where students learn best.*
>
> **In this chapter you will:**
> 1. Read a scenario describing a prime example of the happy and hardworking classroom.
> 2. Think about the type of classroom you currently have compared to the one you would like to have.
> 3. Learn about my five-part philosophy of education that is the foundation for this book.
> 4. Develop your own philosophy of education.

*As you enter Mrs. Miner's sixth grade classroom the first thing you notice is that all students are on task. Students are everywhere but all seem to be engaged in the learning target set forth by the teacher. Moreover, everyone seems happy! Students sit close to one another, smile often, and their quiet whispers are often punctuated by laughter.*

*The room is clearly arranged to meet learners' various needs. About half of the tables at the center of the room are filled with small groups of students talking quietly as they work on gathering and sharing information for a project. There are three study carrels on the back wall with signs above them that read, "Shhhh! Quiet Study Area!" One of the carrels houses a child who is independently reading and taking notes from an article.*

*Along another wall is a tall table with barstools for seating; there, students are working in groups of two with laptops open. Mrs. Miner's desk is in the far back corner of the room but it is empty. She sits at a kidney-shaped table near the front door working with three students. You notice that she occasionally points to the chart on the wall behind her to emphasize a point.*

*When Mrs. Miner needs the attention of her class, she rings a bell and raises her hand. In seconds, all students but one turn toward her. Mrs. Miner politely asks the one student who has not come to attention to please follow directions. The student apologizes and looks at Mrs. Miner. She shares information with the students and asks for volunteers to summarize the work they have done. Many hands shoot up, as students are eager to share. In sharing, students are attentive, ask each other follow-up questions, make connections with one another, and often laugh.*

*As students finish up, Mrs. Miner asks them to put away their work and get ready for lunch. When the children get in line, Mrs. Miner puts a hand on shoulders here and there and stops to chat with individuals who want to share one last thing with her. As she walks them to lunch, she smiles and wishes all a nice break.*

## The Big Idea

Most teachers would love to have a classroom like the one described above. It is a classroom that buzzes with cheery productivity, and that type of classroom is wonderful for all who have a stake in it. From teachers and students to parents and administrators, everyone wins when classrooms are focused on learning, yet joyful. Mrs. Miner's classroom is an example of a place where learning and joy go hand in hand, and that is what this book is all about.

In a nutshell, the theory of this book is that the most effective classrooms are those where students and teachers alike are happy and hardworking. Having spent 22 years as a teacher and curriculum coach in a wide variety of grade levels and schools, I have come to realize that the best classrooms are those that have heady doses of both fun and high expectations.

## My Five-part Philosophy

What is your philosophy of education? This was the question a professor asked in the second year of my teacher education undergraduate program. Philosophy of education? I had no idea. In fact, it wasn't until very recently that my philosophy was anything but an inchoate slush of ideas, inclinations,

> **Your Turn!**
> - ★ Reread the scenario that describes Mrs. Miner's classroom. What did it look like, sound like, and feel like for the students and the teacher? Think about what you would like your own classroom to look like, sound like, and feel like. Use the chart below to jot notes about your hopes for your classroom.
>
> | Looks Like 👁 | Sounds Like 👂 | Feels Like ♡ |
> |---|---|---|
> |  |  |  |
>
> - ★ Ask a trusted colleague to observe your classroom (or video record a lesson or two). Compare your thoughts about what your classroom looks like, sounds like, and feels like to the comments from your observer.
> - ★ Note any gaps between your hopes and the current reality in your room. Think about what you can do to close those gaps.

and questions. Though I know that my philosophy will grow and change, almost 25 years after that question was asked, I think I have an answer.

I have taught grades 1, 2, 4, 5, and 7 and remedial classes in high school. I have worked as a mentor, a cooperating teacher, a professional development coordinator, a reading specialist, and a librarian. Among other places, I have loved students in tiny Yupik villages on the Bering Sea Coast, in inner city Las Vegas, and in rural Wisconsin. I have sat on every possible type of committee and attended more meetings than anyone should ever have to attend. I earned National Board Certification, published in journals, presented at conferences, and embraced the connective power of the internet to grow my own personal and professional learning networks. Most importantly, each year I have loved my profession more deeply and each year has been seminal in my growth as an educator and as an educational philosopher.

Today my philosophy boils down to a list of five things I know to be true about teaching and learning. In my experience, these are among the most important truths for successful educators.

> **The Five-part Philosophy**
> 1. Every single student can grow, learn, and achieve at high levels. All students should be offered a rigorous curriculum that focuses on growth.
> 2. Joy is critical for learning. When students are joyful, they will take more risks, meet more challenges, and generally learn better.
> 3. The best teachers are coaches, not facilitators or bosses.
> 4. Motivation is key, but the way we think of motivation must change.
> 5. Classroom management is absolutely foundational to teaching and learning.

Now that you've taken a minute to read through the five-part philosophy, let's look at each point in greater depth.

> 1. *Every single student can grow, learn, and achieve at high levels. All students should be offered a rigorous curriculum that focuses on growth.*
>
>    All children want to learn and all crave challenge. Students thrive when they work to meet challenging goals in supportive learning environments. So-called "failure is a part of learning and should be celebrated as part of the process." Later in the book, you will read about the research on growth mindset by Carol Dweck (2017), as well as encounter the scholarship on harnessing the power of "failure" as a way to help students recognize themselves as active learners.
>
>    Students with teachers who support the goal of helping them make at least a year's growth in a year's time are bound to achieve more than are students in classrooms where no such expectation is maintained. Take reading in a fifth grade classroom, for example. A student who begins the year reading approximately at the seventh grade level should be challenged to grow to approxi-

> **Identifying a Philosophy of Education Can Help Teachers:**
> - ★ Focus their efforts on what they believe is truly important.
> - ★ Stay true to their core values.
> - ★ Rejuvenate their love of teaching and remind them why they became a teacher in the first place.
> - ★ Make decisions about whether a given school will be a good fit for them.
> - ★ Find allies and thought partners to widen their professional connections.

mately the eighth grade level by year's end. Similarly, a student who begins fifth grade at a second grade reading level should be challenged and supported such that she reaches at least at the third grade level. Both learners should be coached so that they work hard and celebrate their own successes and actually make documented growth.

2  *Joy is critical for learning. When students are joyful, they will take more risks, meet more challenges, and generally learn better.*

Students are in school for a huge chunk of every day. Teachers can and should be actively working to make that time as joyful as possible. When students are happy, they are likely to be motivated to work harder.

Don't make the mistake of thinking that a joyful classroom is equivalent to a free-for-all environment. Remember, the premise of this book is that joy and serious learning go hand in hand. Joyful classrooms can look and sound very different depending on the teacher, the lesson, or even the time of day.
While games, jokes, and other fun can be a part of a joyful classroom, so can a productive buzz or even a completely silent learning space.

3  *The best teachers are coaches, not facilitators or bosses.*

*Coaching* can be defined as the art and science of helping someone achieve their goals through explicit teaching, modeling, hands-on guided practice, and lots of independent practice. Teachers cannot *make* learning happen; they can, however, *help* students acquire knowledge, skills, and tools so that students can make it happen for themselves.

The coaching model places the students' learning efforts at the center of the classroom, while preserving and valuing the teacher's expertise in guiding, troubleshooting, and supporting those efforts. Look to the box below for a comparison of the teacher as boss, facilitator, and coach.

| Teacher Model | Teacher's Role |
| --- | --- |
| **Boss** | Provide direct instruction, act as a "sage on the stage," manage students |
| **Facilitator** | Set up learning experiences, help students as needed, offer very limited direct instruction if any at all |
| **Coach** | Provide direct instruction, facilitate student practice, help students set and meet goals |

4   *Motivation is key, but the way we think of motivation must change.*
    Motivation comes from success and from feeling good about your work; it comes from "seeing" growth through setting, monitoring, and meeting learning goals. Motivation is not something we give to students; it is something we teach to students.
    Real motivation comes from seeing success as possible. Recognition and celebration of growth toward goals should be frequent and pointed. Sometimes, that means a sticker, a certificate, a star on a chart or some other token, but most of the time it means conferring with students so that they begin to see the results of their own hard work to learn and grow.

5   *Classroom management is absolutely foundational to teaching and learning.*
    Unless a teacher has her or his finger on the pulse of the classroom and can easily facilitate student transitions, stay organized, keep disruptive behavior to a minimum, and have fun, she or he cannot effectively teach.
    If students are to make progress in their own areas of need, teachers must be able to flexibly differentiate instruction so that all learners have access to rigorous content in a safe and orderly environment. Differentiated instruction has a reciprocal relationship with classroom management.

Now you have a good idea of my philosophy of education. As you read the rest of the book, you will see that each of the five parts are woven into the chapters to come.

Knowing and being able to articulate your philosophy can be a very helpful touchstone for a teacher. Once we have identified what we believe is truly important, we can weigh our actions, lessons, and approaches against those ideals. If a teacher is doing something that does not feel impactful in light of her or his philosophy, there might be a problem, and problems can be fixed when we can pinpoint them.

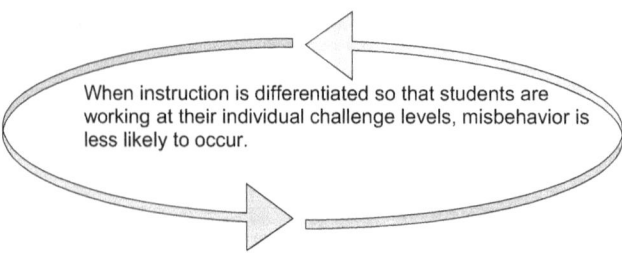

**Figure 1.1** The reciprocal relationship between differentiated instruction and classroom management.

> **Your Turn!**
> - ★ Do you agree with the five-part philosophy? What would you change to make it better fit your own experiences and beliefs about what constitutes good teaching?
> - ★ Define your own philosophy of learning. Ask yourself the following questions and use the answers to guide you.
>   1. What do you hold most dear as a teacher?
>   2. What truths guide how you interact with your students?
>   3. What was your best experience as a student? As a teacher?
>   4. What is your biggest hope for your students?
>   5. What do you think works in teaching and learning? What doesn't work?

## How to Read This Book

This book is designed to be very practical. Each chapter is resource-rich, with an emphasis on strategies that can be immediately implemented to help you in your quest to become a teacher in a happy and hardworking classroom (or even happier and more hardworking, if you already have one!).

The strategies are grounded in the research, scholarship, and evidence base offered by leaders in education and from practical and effective classroom teachers.

Each chapter is laid out in a consistent manner that includes the following features:

- ◆ A preview of the learning targets for the chapter.
- ◆ The big idea or the "whats and whys" of the topic.
- ◆ Research highlights, the scholarship, and the evidence base that the chapter is founded on.
- ◆ Simple tips, hints, and ideas for implementation.
- ◆ Ideas to try.
- ◆ A review of the chapter's main points.

As you read the book, I hope you will find that each chapter is braided into the rest. In reading through the chapter summaries below, I think you'll see that the big ideas flow in and out of each section.

*Chapter 1: Working Hard, Working Happy*
As you know by now, this first chapter serves as an introduction to the book. The focus will be explaining the underlying five-part philosophy

of learning that gives way to the methods and strategies offered in the subsequent chapters.

### *Chapter 2: Joy and Effort, Best Friends Forever!*

The most effective classrooms are those where students and teachers alike are happy and hardworking. This chapter will focus on the whats and whys of a high-functioning classroom. Here, the relationships between fun, high levels of self-efficacy, personal satisfaction, rigor, and student effort will be explored. The chapter is organized around Daniel Pink's notions of purpose, mastery, and autonomy/ownership.

### *Chapter 3: Where Everyone Knows Your Name*

Happy classrooms, where all students are willing to take risks and challenge themselves, begin with a foundation of strong relationships between all stakeholders in the classroom. Teachers and students must know and respect each other, and that must also be true between students. Building relationships, a strong foundation of classroom management, and a culture of caring will be addressed with the overarching goal of building safe classrooms for all learners. Without a safe, respectful classroom, learning is not likely to happen.

### *Chapter 4: Mastery Matters!*

Motivation can hinge on students seeing themselves as capable of mastery. Once students learn to set and meet goals, they will begin to see themselves as successful and autonomous learners. Helping students see their own learning will make the classroom happier and more productive. This chapter will explore strategies to build students' abilities to master material and to see themselves making progress.

### *Chapter 5: Have It Your Way! Differentiated Instruction*

If students are to be successful, then teachers must learn to differentiate instruction in meaningful and varied ways. This chapter will help teachers explore ways to differentiate instruction such that all students are working toward rigorous learning goals within their own zones of proximal development.

### *Chapter 6: Social Animals*

Students, like all human beings, are social animals. This chapter will help readers to harness that social drive and energy through various formal and informal cooperative learning techniques. When students work together and have a shared vision, they are likely to be happier. That can help a teacher to motivate all to work hard and learn with and from each other.

*Chapter 7: Busting Down the Walls, Building Community Connections*
In addition to feeling known by the teacher, students who are taught by teachers who are integrated into the community and have frequent and positive interactions with parents are likely to work harder and experience the classroom as a joyful place. This chapter will focus on helping teachers to reach out and support the community at large and, in turn, receive support from it.

*Chapter 8: Effort and Joy, They're Not Just for Students!*
Teachers have a hard job. If it is to be a doable and long-lasting career, then we must do two things. One, point our efforts in the most impactful direction and, two, increase and sustain joy in our working lives.

---

**Recapping the BIG Idea**

*Classrooms that develop a culture of joy and effort are classrooms where students learn best.*

**In this chapter we looked at:**
1. The philosophies that I believe guide the happy and hardworking classroom.
2. The importance of having a sense of how you want your classroom to look, sound, and feel.
3. The idea of developing your own philosophy of education.

---

## Reference

Dweck, C. S. (2017). *Mindset*. London: Robinson, an imprint of Constable & Robinson Ltd.

# 2

# Joy and Effort, Best Friends Forever!

> **The BIG Idea**
> *Joy and hard work go hand in hand in a teacher's efforts to motivate students to meet learning goals.*
>
> **In this chapter you will:**
> 1. Understand how joy matters to learning.
> 2. Connect working hard with joy.
> 3. Identify the drivers of self-motivated learning.
> 4. Discover the relationship between joy, self-efficacy, personal satisfaction, and rigor.
> 5. Learn strategies to help you increase motivation, hard work, and joy in your classroom.

## The Theory and Research

Before digging deeper into the evidence base that makes the case for the happy and hardworking classroom, take a minute and reflect on the following questions.

- Do you believe that joy/happiness is important for day-to-day and/or long-term learning?
- Is your classroom/school a joyful/happy place?

- Do you believe that students can and want to work hard in your class?
- Is your classroom a place where students are asked and inspired to work hard?

I hope you were able to answer "yes" to most of these questions, and if not, I hope you want to soon be able to answer them "yes."

## Joy Matters!

In this book, the words happiness and joy and their derivatives will be used interchangeably and mean a positive, pervasive, and long-term state of being. *Joy* and *happiness* are used to describe the general climate and culture of the school or classroom. While the idea of *fun* is an important component of a joyful classroom, it is not synonymous. Why? Because fun is a temporary state of being or doing and, as noted above, joy and happiness connote a long-term sense of well-being that is present even when a person is not having fun.

For example, students might have fun in class while playing a game, watching a funny video, or working as a team to complete a challenge. That type of fun is valuable and ultimately helps build the joyful classroom we should all strive for. However, in a truly joyful classroom, students feel happy even when the work they are engaged in is not immediately fun.

For example, students who are working hard on a math test or a writing assignment, or are reading quietly, feel good about their work, positive about their environment, and basically happy to be in school even though they may not be laughing or showing other overt indications of having fun. Read the scenarios below to further your understanding of the difference between a joyful classroom and a fun classroom.

*Mr. Mark (not his real name), a fourth grade teacher at our school, is what some would call a "strict" teacher. He is precise with his instructions, routines, and expectations for student behavior. His classroom rules and the consequences for breaking them are clear to students. Though students rarely test Mr. Mark, when they do, they find that consequences are quickly and fairly applied. A visitor to his classroom would think of the environment as old-fashioned. The desks are all in rows, the students are quiet, and Mr. Mark monitors work from his desk. Effort, independence, and quality workmanship are all valued, and the students truly want to meet expectations and please their teacher.*

*Mr. Mark clearly cares about all of his students and has a nickname for most. When he calls students to his desk to confer with them about their work, the students stand close to him and hang on his every word. They beam with pride from a compliment and nod their heads to show understanding when he shares corrective feedback with him.*

*From time-to-time, Mr. Mark is very purposeful in injecting fun into his classroom. Students sometimes get an extra recess or have whole-class competitions from bingo to spelling bees. At the end of the day, every student gives Mr. Mark an "elbow bump" as a sign of affection and togetherness. When the school does their yearly climate survey, students consistently report that they are happy in Mr. Mark's care. Moreover, students who are not in Mr. Mark's class because they were assigned another teacher or are not yet old enough to be there often comment that they wish they were in his class. The icing on the cake? Academic indicators of achievement are high, and students in Mr. Mark's care tend to do slightly better on standardized measures of reading and math achievement than do those in other classrooms.*

While Mr. Mark's kind of classroom might not be one that is typically thought of as fun – and in fact is sometimes denigrated in educational literature as old-fashioned – it is effective and the students are happy. He is active in the community as a coach and sports enthusiast and students truly appreciate him and feel appreciated by him.

Contrast Mr. Mark's happy and hardworking classroom with the following scenario, which depicts a colleague of his in the same grade, at the same school. Note that this colleague, here called Mrs. Kerkowsky, has a very different style but an equally joyful and hardworking group of students.

*Mrs. Kerkowsky's room is sometimes described as productive chaos. The classroom uses a flexible seating model, and during small group work sessions students are everywhere! Some are even outside of the classroom in the hallway, lying on the floor with clipboards. They are working on multi-step math problems. The groups all have different problems built around the same mathematical concept. Students are boisterous as they work, and there is frequent laughter. Mrs. Kerkowsky wanders between groups, hunkering down beside each to check progress, offer feedback, and occasionally remind students that "It's okay to have fun, guys, but you really need to focus on the work. This problem will really get your brain going and we're just getting started today!"*

*The area behind Mrs. Kerkowsky's desk is filled with evidence that students adore her. There are hand-drawn pictures, notes, and signs, all which, in one way or another, make it clear that her students are happy to be in her class. Mrs. Kerkowsky frequently surveys her students and their parents about how they feel the year is going. Survey results invariably show that her learners and their parents are happy with her work. Measures of standardized achievement prove that Mrs. Kerkowsky's methods are effective as the students in her care consistently outperform the national average, and individuals make tremendous growth in reading and math.*

Mr. Mark and Mrs. Kerkowsky are based on real teachers that I work with. They have very different approaches to teaching and learning. But, in both rooms, students are happy and hardworking. Though Mrs. Kerkowsky's class might seem more fun and Mr. Mark's class might seem more work-focused, the survey and academic data indicate that both offer joyful environments with rigorous learning expectations that hinge on student effort.

I have observed classrooms all across the continuums for over 20 years and have learned that joy and rigor can take many different forms, and there are many different teacher styles or approaches that work to create happy classrooms. The point? When I talk about joyful learning environments, I do so with the intention of including teachers with different philosophies and classroom management styles. Joyful classrooms can be cultivated with teachers who infuse daily doses of silly, playful, sometimes even wild fun (I am that type of teacher) or with teachers who run a tight and orderly ship but do so with love and respect for the students they teach (Mr. Mark is that type of teacher).

No matter a teacher's style, joy is critical for success. Joyful classroom environments help students learn better, and that's the whole point, right? While it may seem obvious that happy students learn, it is more than just common sense; it is also backed by research. Studies show that joy matters in school.

- According to neuroscientist Martha Burns (2012), dopamine is released when we experience joy. Dopamine, in lay terms, is a chemical in the brain that is involved in controlling the brain's pleasure and reward centers. When dopamine is released, it acts like an intrinsic reward system. Burns refers to dopamine as a "save button," because when it is released, it provokes development of long-term memory.
- When humor is interjected into lessons, students are more likely to retain what they've learned, are likely to be less stressed, and are more primed to be resilient. This is because when teachers joke with students, it can help engage them and keep their attention. Of course, humor also helps make the entire classroom environment more inviting (Stambor, 2006).
- In classrooms that are perceived as fun, a sense of community is developed and students' affective filters are lowered (Edwards, 2010). The term *affective filter* comes from a hypothesis offered by language acquisition scholar Stephen Krashen (1995). The hypothesis is that there are affective elements – mood, feelings, and attitudes – that make learning easier or harder depending on how negative or positive the affective elements are.
- When students feel fear, pressure, low self-esteem, or anger, new ideas cannot pass through the affective filter and students cannot learn optimally.

New Ideas 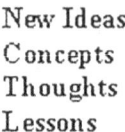  Fear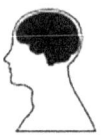
Concepts              Pressure
Thoughts              Low Self-Esteem
Lessons               Anger

Figure 2.1 Negative thoughts can block new learning.

- Conversely, Krashen posited that when students feel positive, motivated, at ease, and confident, their affective filter is low. When the filter is low, students are more susceptible to new ideas, taking risks, and learning. The key is to make sure that your classroom is not setting up a negative affective filter for learners.

### Simple Tips, Hints, and Ideas to Increase Joy

Truly, every chapter in the book offers strategies to make your classroom more joyful. Below are easy-to-implement tips, hints, and ideas to bolster the work you do to make your classroom a happy place.

To increase the culture of joy in your classroom, start by focusing on three things:

1. Smiling often,
2. Laughing more, and
3. Being kind to yourself.

The bottom line is that the teacher is the leader in her or his classroom and thus sets the tone. If you want students to be happy and your classroom to be joyful, it is imperative that you model that for the children in your care. My husband often comments on the fact that a smile is my default facial expression. I cannot imagine a better compliment. The truth is that over the years, I have worked hard to make it that way. Smiles are warm and inviting. They make us look approachable, and that is exactly what I want.

Let's be honest, we don't always feel joyful at school. Sometimes a smile is hard to find, never mind honest laughter. But, as most teachers know, students reflect the attitudes we put out. Given the science, we want our students to be joyful, and thus we must learn to skillfully cultivate joy in ourselves. Teachers deserve a joyful environment too! It's not only the kids who are in school for a large part of every day. It is not only the students who are learning. So, how do we learn to smile and laugh more? Read on!

1   Don't feel it? Fake it, until you make it by "acting as if . . ."
    Years ago I had an incredible mentor who helped me see my role as the culture leader in my classroom. Once, after a night spent bailing floodwater from my basement, I came to school tired and grumpy and ready to frown through the day. My mentor, who did not mince words, said, "It's okay to feel grumpy and to be tired. It's not okay for you to put that mood on your room full of kids."

    She reminded me that it is my *job* to put things aside and jump into the joy of teaching. To *fake it*. To *act as if* I was joyful. What she didn't tell me was that by putting on a smile, forcing myself to tell a joke and to laugh, and basically pretending to be joyful, I actually became joyful!

    Don't get me wrong, I'm not saying a fake smile is a cure for depression, or that it made me happier about my flooded basement. I am saying that during the workday, teachers have the chance to lift up or bring down our students. We must choose to lift them up. Smile. Laugh. Act as if.

2   Laugh at your own jokes
    Even when they're not funny, jokes are fun! When I taught seventh grade language arts, I started each unit with a joke. For example, before I started a study of science fiction, I told the following joke:
    – *So, yesterday, I went to visit my husband in his man-cave. It was a mess. Among the piles of papers, books, and balled up dirty laundry, I found an ugly creature lying dead on the floor. I asked my husband what it was. He said, "It's an alien." I replied, "Oh it must have been one of those brain-suckers. Too bad he found* your *room first. It looks like he starved to death!"*

    Again, perhaps not the funniest joke in the world, but it served its purpose. And in addition to the giggles, outright laughter (and, okay, some groans), I had every student's eyes on me when I said, "Guess what genre we're going to study next?"
    Don't know any jokes? Google them. In fact, stop reading this book and google a joke to start your upcoming units right now.

3   Play music
    When I feel boredom or exhaustion creeping into class, or when I see kids need to take a break, or I note a need to celebrate, I transform into DJ Crazy-Teacher.
    Throwing a two-minute dance party is a great way to bring the joy. There is nothing like music and movement to elevate a mood. Try it. I defy anyone to listen to Sam and the Womp sing *Bom, Bom*, or Katrina and the Waves sing *Walking on Sunshine*, and not feel happy. Really, it's a challenge! Stop reading and dial them up on YouTube right now. Instant

mood elevation! Make your own Happy Playlist and share it with kids or use it between classes when you're priming yourself for full-on class fun. If that's not your style, even playing peaceful, calming music while students work quietly can increase joy. As a child of the 70s, I often play classic rock or folk music in the background. My students know and love the Steve Miller Band, Bob Dylan, Joni Mitchell, Van Morrison, and others and even ask for them by name.

4  YouTube it

Cute babies, grumpy cats, and funny memes can all work wonders. It's easy to find good stuff pretty quickly with Google Images and YouTube. Try watching the funny version of *School Rules with the Minions* or *Kid Snippets* on learning math. Both are easily accessible with a quick search and both are really funny!

Oddly, even when videos aren't funny, they can feel like a treat for students. Using TeacherTube, Khan Academy, BrainPop, or other sources for academic videos allows teachers to learn alongside the class and can increase positive feelings.

I'll let you in on a little secret. I sometimes record videos of myself teaching lessons, split my students into two groups and ultimately team-teach with myself. The students love it! They are incredibly engaged with video-me and seem to learn better from her. Similarly, they enjoy working with me in a smaller group when it's their turn for real-me. The bonus is that many students rewatch the video lessons at home!

5  Use games and technology

Adding games to the curriculum is a great way to up the fun-factor in your classroom, which can, of course, lead to long-term joy. There are so many wonderful online learning games that teachers can use to help students learn, practice, or review academic concepts. Below are suggestions for easy-to-use and free tools to make learning fun with technology.

- *Kahoot!* (https://kahoot.com/) Kahoot! is an online platform where teachers can make a quiz-show-type game. The teacher broadcasts the quiz show on an interactive whiteboard or with a projector. Students play in teams or in one-on-one competitions. Even better, Kahoot! games can be played in real time with students all over the world. I have made many games with Kahoot!, including a review of nonfiction text features, states and capitals, and literary devices used in fiction. In all cases, students had fun, and I was able to identify gaps in learning.
- *Goosechase* (www.goosechase.com/) Using this tool in connection with iPads, teachers can create scavenger hunts where students

explore different environments and take pictures of items that help them prove they understand content. I worked with an art teacher to create a Goosechase scavenger hunt, in which students took pictures of elements of art (shapes, space, line, texture, etcetera) they found at a local sculpture park.
- *JeopardyLabs* (https://jeopardylabs.com/) Here teachers can quickly and easily create online jeopardy games. Even better, hand over the power to students who can create review games for their peers.
- *EdPuzzle* (https://edpuzzle.com/) While not a game, EdPuzzle can be a fun way to meaningfully integrate video into the curriculum. With EdPuzzle, you can choose any video on the web or one you have created yourself, upload it to the EdPuzzle website, and manipulate it to meet your students' learning needs. For example, I often upload spoken-word poetry or short stories and then edit them so that they have just the parts I want students to see. Then, I add multiple choice and short answer questions. Students love working in EdPuzzle, and I like the extra touch of accountability it adds for students as they use videos to learn.
- *Flipgrid* (https://info.flipgrid.com/) Like EdPuzzle, this isn't a game platform, but a way to harness the power of video to make learning fun. Free for teachers, Flipgrid allows users to record very short videos and lets them respond to other users' videos as well. I have used Flipgrid to get students talking about everything from their favorite books to how they solved a math problem. In one project, I opened up the Flipgrid to users worldwide, and my students were able to chat with other learners near and far.

6  Practice gratitude

Focusing what makes us grateful can help build overall well-being. Years ago, I kept a gratitude journal (as Oprah suggested). Each evening I wrote a list of things that happened that day or that were pervasive in my life that I was thankful for. It really did help keep me feeling positive. When I had my own kids and could no longer find the time to continue with the journal, I let the entire concept of conscientious gratitude slip aside. Then, last year, I read a wonderful book, *First Aid for Teacher Burnout* by Dr. Jenny Rankin (2017). Dr. Rankin wrote, "Countless studies recount the power of gratitude, so consider daily recalling ways in which you are blessed. If you are burned out, better days are surely ahead because you are taking positive steps to make it so" (p. 15).

I decided to bring habits of gratitude back to my daily life. Because I wash my hands up to 10 times each day (you're a teacher – you know

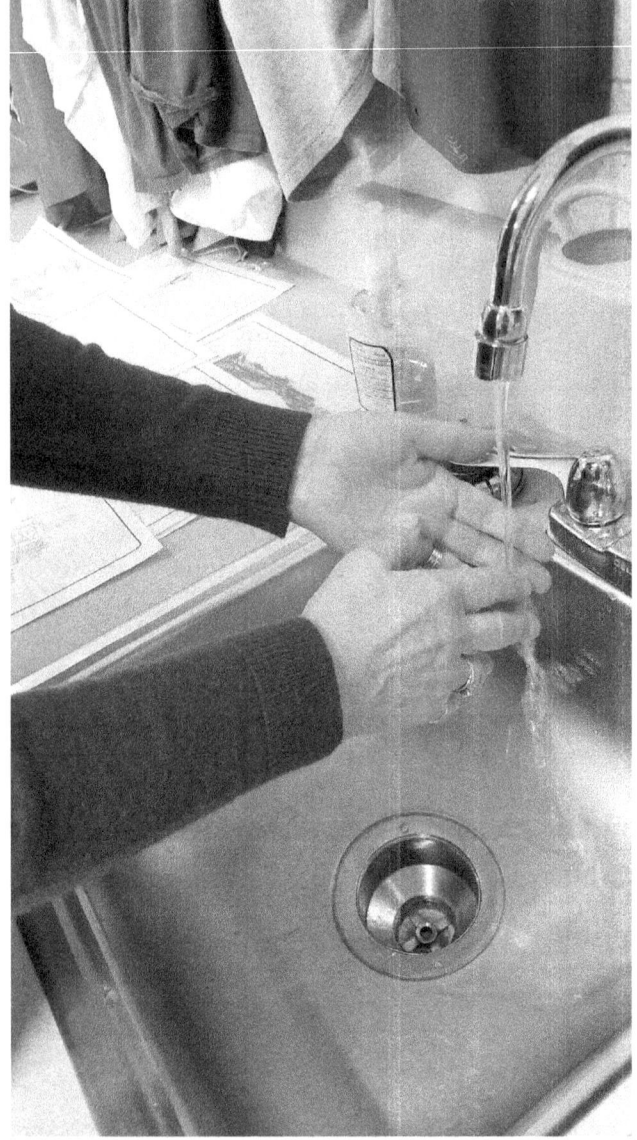

Image 2.1 Frequent handwashing keeps your body and mind healthy and happy.

how germy schools can be), I decided to use each handwashing as a time to think about things and people I am grateful for. I quickly formed a habit and have found the practice of "grateful handwashing" to be enriching.

## Hard Work Matters Too!

Of course, it's not all about sunshine and rainbows. At its very best, joy in the classroom serves to increase achievement. Almost anyone who knows me as

> **Your Turn!**
> - What are you already doing to make your classroom or school a joyful place?
> - What could you do to make it more joyful?
> - What are you doing to be kind to yourself?
> - What could you do to be even kinder?
> - What new fun tech idea can you meaningfully integrate into your teaching?

a teacher knows that when it comes to learning, I am serious. I hold my students to high standards just as I do myself. Students in my classes understand that demonstrating academic growth is the bottom line. Put in other words, as I tell my students, smiles, laughter, and fun are a *part* of hard work, *not* the opposite of it. Put even more strongly, I believe that when students work hard in a supportive environment, that hard work pays off in lasting joy.

## What Rigor is, What Rigor is NOT

For many, hard work, growth-focused learning, and rigor are synonymous. However, in recent times, the word *rigor* has been tainted with a connotation that I don't like. Rigor too often is code for arbitrarily defined expectations that seem to be intentionally placed above a child's actual ability. Rigor has replaced the infinitely better concept of allowing students to work and learn within their comfort level and slightly above *with* support from teachers, peers, and parents and through differentiated assignments (more on differentiation in Chapter 5).

Rigor should be defined based on an individual's learning needs. Rigor should not mean *hard*. It should mean instruction, schoolwork, learning experiences, and education expectations that are academically, intellectually, and personally challenging – but not consistently frustrating and not just more work. Rigor should call on students to put forth effort to learn while respecting their unique learning needs.

Barbara Blackburn (2017) has written extensively about the concept of rigor. She shares four myths surrounding the concept.

Rigor does not mean

1. More homework.
2. More in-school work.
3. Only for gifted students.
4. Lessened by differentiated work or levels of teacher support.

Blackburn says, "True rigor is expecting every student to learn and perform at high levels and requires that students delve deeply into their learning, engage in critical thinking and problem solving, and be curious and imaginative." (Blackburn, 2017).

Some educators are opting to use the word *vigor* in place of rigor. Leader Michael Fisher (2016) wrote about it by reminding that rigor connotes rigidity, severity, and strict adherence, not something most teachers want associated with their classrooms, especially those who are interested in cultivating a joyful classroom. As an alternative, Fisher offers *vigor* as a replacement, because vigor brings to mind enthusiasm, energy, and flourishing growth.

In this book, rigor means helping students to work hard to grow and learn within their own academic starting places, levels, interests, and needs for support. Using this definition, rigor goes hand in hand with the Gradual Release of Responsibility Model of teaching and learning.

### The GRR and Friends!

The Gradual Release of Responsibility Model is sometimes referred to as the GRR Model or the "I do, We do, You do" Model. The idea is that good teaching and intensive learning usually starts with direct instruction and/or modeling, is followed with guided practice where students use new skills, strategies, and concepts under the guidance of a teacher or another capable coach, and ends with students using the skill, concept, or strategy independently. The model hinges on teachers checking for understanding throughout the entire cycle.

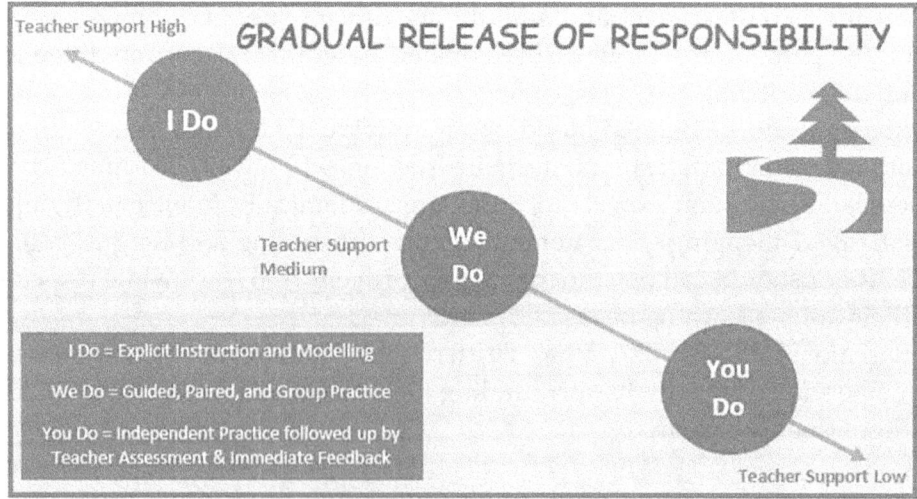

Figure 2.2 The gradual release of responsibility model.

At one end of the model, teacher support is very high and at the other, very low. Look at the graphic and examples below for more on the Gradual Release of Responsibility Model.

*Mrs. Scott is a master teacher. She is ready to teach the students the process of dividing mixed numbers. She knows from years of experience that this can be very difficult for her students. As she develops her lessons, she uses the GRR Model to help her plan to meet their needs.*

**"I do": model and direct instruction.** *In her first lesson, Mrs. Scott begins by saying,* "Class, you have come a long way in your ability to think mathematically and I'm excited to tell you that we are ready to start a new challenge. We're going to learn how to divide mixed numbers." *She then shows a video of the process.* "As you watch," *she says,* "Think about how what you see reminds you of skills you already have." *While the students watch, Mrs. Scott walks around the classroom, helping to keep students focused and watching for subtle cues, from furrowed brows to head nods that help her identify who is "getting it" and who might need extra support. As the video ends, Mrs. Scott asks students to turn to a partner and share their thoughts on what skills they already have in place that will help with dividing mixed numbers. After this brief discussion, Mrs. Scott asks students to open their texts so that they can follow along as she models working through the practice problems. After doing three practice problems, she does a quick check for understanding, asking her students to put their thumb up if they feel ready to try on their own, their thumb sideways if they feel they can try but aren't confident that they will be successful, and their thumb down if they feel they still don't get it.*

**"We do": guided practice.** *Mrs. Scott uses this quick thumb-check for understanding to move into the next phase of the lesson. To the students who gave a thumbs-up, she says,* "Please find a partner who had a thumb-sideways. Sit and work through practice problems 1–5. I will come by frequently to check on you and ask questions." *She knows that pairing students who feel they have solid understanding with those who have a more tenuous hold will benefit both groups. While these students pair up and get started, Mrs. Scott directs the students who had a thumb down to the kidney table at the back of the room. She uses an iPad to start another video on dividing mixed numbers. This one is from the online version of their math program. She tells students to watch it and that she will return in a few minutes to work through the practice problems with them as a group. As the students at the kidney table view the second video, Mrs. Scott walks through the classroom from group to group checking for progress, correcting misconceptions, and offering praise to student pairs. As the video ends, she returns to the small group. She asks students to rate their understanding again. All now show a sideways or a thumbs-up. She asks them all to work through practice problem 1 and she watches and offers corrective* *feedback as they do. As they move to the next problem, she rotates through the class again and sees that all are on track.*

**"You do": independent practice.** *Once Mrs. Scott feels confident that all students have made progress up the learning curve, she is ready for them to enter the "you do" phase of independent practice. She assigns three problems as homework. The next day, she quickly checks the problems while the students complete two more as a part of their beginning of class seat work. She will use the results to inform the math lesson later in the period and in the coming days.*

Education scholars Douglas Fisher and Nancy Frey (2014) and Regie Routman (2018) offer two innovations to the GRR Model.

For the purposes of pointing out augmentations to the GRR Model offered by Fisher and Frey, I will refer to their version of GRR as GRR+. The plus sign indicates a vital addition to GRR. In GRR+, students work together to help each other as an important part of the learning process.

> *Unfortunately, most current efforts to implement the gradual release of responsibility framework limit these interactions to adult and child exchanges: I do it; we do it together; you do it. But this three-phase model omits a truly vital component: students learning through collaboration with their peers – the* you do it together *phase.*
>
> (Fisher & Frey, 2014, p. 3, emphasis in original)

Thus, the model becomes, "I do," "We do," "You children do it together," and "You do it yourself."

Routman (2018) suggests using what she calls the Optimal Learning Model (OLM). The OLM continues to focus on teachers and students working together to learn, but while the GRR tends to focus on the teacher's behaviors, the OLM focuses on those of the students. Routman points out that the OLM is best seen as a cycle, writing, "the learning process is fluid and recursive, not linear or rigid" (p. 137).

The OLM has a strong focus on using assessment to drive what lesson planning (including what phase of OLM) should be employed. From a very practical perspective, an important difference between OLM and GRR is that in the OLM there are two "we do" components. The first stage is very much led by the teacher giving directions while the students do the work and the second stage is the opposite, students do the work and lead the way. This can have a positive effect on the pacing of a lesson, because it can, when necessary, slow the process of handing over responsibility to students when needed. Rather than jumping from guided practice to independent work too quickly, there is an added, flexible step.

> **Your Turn!**
> - How do the GRR, GRR+, and the OLM compare with how you design lessons?
> - How do the GRR, GRR+, and the OLM fit with the five-part philosophy shared in Chapter 1?

## Motivation Theory

There is perhaps no stronger support for the relationship between hard work and joy than the research on motivation. Students who are highly motivated are most likely to find school to be a joyful place and to happily work hard. So, how do we motivate our learners? In Chapter 4, I will offer details and ideas on how to motivate students to do their best. A basic understanding of motivation theory is offered below. Dan Pink (2012), author of *Drive: The Surprising Truth about What Motivates Us*, explains the basics of motivation in his very readable book summarizing the research and evidence.

Pink is a journalist who aggregated the research on motivation and came to illuminating conclusions. His book is excellent. It is well worth a read, but if you can't find the time, I encourage you to at least watch the 10-minute video of him talking about his work. Pink's *RSA Animate* video is easy to find on the web and well worth a watch or two (or in my case, more than 20!). It has nearly 17 million views! Yup, it's that good!

In a nutshell, Pink says that in order to be motivated, a person must have autonomy or choice, a clear purpose for what they are doing, and the perception that they can achieve mastery. Look below for a more detailed explanation of each factor.

> **Autonomy + Purpose + Mastery = Motivated Learners!**

*Autonomy:* Autonomy means allowing for maximum self-determination. In the classroom, autonomy can manifest in offering students voice and choice (these concepts will be further explored in Chapter 5). In the example of Mrs. Scott's classroom above, allowing students to self-assess their understanding with thumb-checks gave them a measure of autonomy in making decisions about their own learning needs. Other examples of autonomy are allowing students to choose where they sit and offering options for how to complete work or demonstrate understanding.

*Purpose:* Purpose is about helping students understand why what they are learning is important, how it relates to what they have already learned and will learn in future lessons, and to "real life." Mrs. Scott connected prior learning to the new concept of dividing mixed numbers. Helping students see the purpose for what they are learning is as easy as stating purpose at the beginning of your lesson. I start most lessons by asking and answering the following questions with students.

- What am I learning?
- Why am I learning it?
- How will I know when I've learned it?

I made a colorful mini-poster with those questions, laminated it, and keep it on the stool at the front of my classroom so I see it often. It helps me stay tuned in to "purpose" and making sure to help students understand purpose.

*Mastery:* Mastery means allowing students access to content that they can be successful with and intentionally showing students their success with data and other evidence. In Mrs. Scott's math lesson, students worked through problems both with her support and independently, and in both cases they were offered feedback in a timely manner. When students see themselves learning, they can begin to believe they are capable of mastery.

### The Role of Self-control in Hardworking and Happy Classrooms

Teachers must cultivate balance, and students must learn to walk that fine line between a fun and a wild, off-task classroom. I do that in two ways. First, I remind students of "Grandma's Rule" (while also pointing out that I am in no way old enough to be their grandmother).

Grandma's Rule can be summed up as, "First veggies, then dessert!" When at all possible, the day-to-day work of learning should have dessertish qualities, but my students know that if they want some joy-making craziness, they not only have to be on task and focused most of the time, but they also have to be ready to come right back into the learning zone when the song is over, the video is finished, and the last joke is cracked.

---

**Your Turn!**
- ★ Reflect on your classroom as it relates to Dan Pink's summary of the research on motivation. What are examples of the following in your class?
  1. Student autonomy.
  2. Students' understanding of the purpose of the work they do.
  3. Students' ability to master content and see evidence of their own mastery.
- ★ How might you use Pink's summary of the research on motivation to help your students be more successful?

I cultivate this understanding by challenging students to practice self-control. Some years, I start by blowing up dozens of balloons and leaving them in the classroom. Then, I challenge my students to not touch them, saying, "I love a joyful, fun classroom. But, I also love learning. You are going to learn a lot this year. You're also going to have fun. Today, I want to see how much self-control you have. That's important for me to know before I let my fun side kick in."

Kids get the message right away and, for the most part, they leave the balloons alone. At the end of that first day, I explain Grandma's Rule, and in the last two minutes of that first day of school we go crazy throwing and bouncing balloons and filling our shared space with joy!

Another idea for helping students think about how self-control fits into a hardworking and joyful classroom is to talk with them about the Stanford Marshmallow Test (Mischel, 2015). This was an experiment in which researchers gave young children a marshmallow. The researcher then left the room, telling the children that they could eat the marshmallow now and only get one, or wait for a short time and get two marshmallows when the researcher returned to the room. Children from the study were followed, and results showed that the children with the greatest self-control tended to have more successful lives in terms of academic achievement and other economic and social indicators. A video of the Marshmallow Test can be found on YouTube. Sharing it with your students can be a good jumping-off point for a discussion about self-control.

It is, however, important to note that there have been recent studies that confirm that a child's income level is way more predictive to future success than the ability to delay gratification (Calarco, 2018). These studies replicated the Marshmallow Test using a wider swath of participants and conclusively found that "self-control alone couldn't overcome economic and social disadvantages." This means that richer kids were more successful at holding off on eating the marshmallow than were their poorer counterparts. While wealth as a driving factor in success is certainly proven true, it doesn't mitigate the role of self-control. Most teachers would agree that teaching self-control is important. So, using the Marshmallow Test videos can still be a good way to help youngsters understand the concept of self-control, even though there are conflicting analyses of what the study means in the long run.

## Simple Tips, Hints, and Ideas to Help you Build a Hardworking Classroom

As with the tips to make your classroom more joyful, the entirety of this book will help you increase rigor and motivate students to put forth their best efforts in daily learning. Below are easy-to-implement tips, hints, and ideas to help you build a hardworking classroom.

1 Make learning targets clear

Earlier, the negative connotations associated with the word *rigor* were discussed. I notice a similar issue with the phrase *learning targets* and its various iterations. Mandates associated with learning targets – including posting "I can" statements, "unpacking standards," and an ever-changing vocabulary (*learning targets*, *learning intentions*, *objective*, *essential learnings*, etc.) – have left many teachers with a high level of learning-target fatigue. I have felt that myself. When I asked a colleague about it, here is what he had to say,

— *My skin crawls when I hear the words* I can statements. *I feel like we've been unpacking standards and writing "I can statements" to the exclusion of actually thinking about meeting kids' needs. Why do I have to post my targets here or there? Why do I have to have the same targets as the teacher next door? It irks me. But, at the same time, I know how important it is both for me to know what I'm teaching and for the kids to know what they are supposed to be learning. It's just that the whole concept feels forced because of the way the profession is going about it.*

Fatigue aside, learning targets are important, and we can't let misguided interpretations and arbitrary rules lead us away from sharing them with our students. Helping students see the purpose for the work they do is critical to motivation. Having observed many classrooms in all grades over the course of my career, I know that not only do students often not know *why* they are doing something, they sometimes don't even know *what* they are doing.

In the best-case scenario, a visitor to your class could ask any student what they were learning and why, and every student could answer in a simple way. Of course, that is not possible if learning targets aren't clear. To make them clear, they should be focused on the essential learning embedded in a given standard and stated simply in student-friendly language. They should help teachers and students answer the three questions first shared above. Aside from writing them so they are student-friendly, the format doesn't matter. Write them on the board, post them, ask students to jot them down, or simply state and restate them, whatever seems to work best. Don't let them become rote. As long as your lesson is focused on the target and the students know the target, it will likely impact learning. You will read more about this in Chapter 4.

> **What am I learning?**
> **Why am I learning it?**
> **How will I know when I've learned it?**

2  **Do less but do it better**
   Whenever possible, drop an assignment!
   This tip may seem counterintuitive in a "cover the content" culture. Remember, however, that rigor does not mean *doing more*, it means *appropriately challenging*. If we want students to work hard and do their best as a matter of course, then we have to make sure not only that the tasks we ask them to do are worth doing, but also that students are held to a high standard for doing quality work.

3  **Breed success**
   If students are to work hard, they have to have a sense of themselves as having been successful in the past and see themselves as capable of further success, or as Dan Pink (2012) notes, capable of mastering content. Here are some ways to encourage and highlight success in your classroom.
   - Celebrate successes and post student work. Even older students can get a kick out of a sticker or a star when they've done excellent work. Two-minute dance parties, a handwritten note, or just a pat on the back can all go a long way.
   - Call parents and share positive stories about their children. Carry your cell phone in your pocket and pull it out to call or text when someone does something amazing. When students consent to it, calling parents on the spot and in front of the entire class is fun, exciting, and motivating!
   - When students start new challenges or are struggling, remind them of successes they've had in the past. Similarly, teach students to practice positive self-talk. When they feel nervous or overwhelmed, remind them to think about challenges they conquered, telling themselves, "If I could do that, I can do this too!"
   - Flip "failure on its head." Teach students that failure is often an inevitable part of eventual success. I tell my students to think of FAIL as an acronym that stands for First Attempt In Learning. Of course, this is only true when students put forth effort. Failure without effort is a different story entirely.
   - Emphasize the power of "yet"! Remind students that learning is incremental. When students claim they "can't" do this or that, ask them to add the word *yet* to the proclamation. For example, if a student says, "I can't figure out the answer!" Ask her/him to say, "I can't figure out the answer, yet!"
   
   Remember, success breeds success, and success is a powerful motivator.

4  **Teach growth mindset**

Growth mindset refers to the theory that intelligence and ability are changeable rather than fixed. Researcher Carol Dweck (2017) spent years studying intelligence and has concluded that people can actually make themselves smarter through effort. Her studies have been borne out on IQ tests; people have seen their IQ scores raised by several points! As teachers, we need to convince ourselves and our students that every human being is capable of actually growing their intelligence. This is important for motivation. If students and their teachers have growth mindsets, they are inherently motivated to achieve more.

One important aspect of growth mindset is praising effort over ability. Instead of calling students "smart" when they do well, try saying, "Well done! You worked hard on this!"

5  **Brand your classroom**

In Chapter 1, you read about developing a guiding philosophy. Once you have done that, it is time to brand your classroom! The concept of "branding" has been around in the business world for years, but has only recently made its way into education circles. Branding is the practice of developing a unique identity for your product – in this case, your classroom. When something is branded, hearing its name immediately generates pictures in your mind, with positive and very specific associations. For example, when you think of Apple products or see their logo, you probably think of stylish designs and ease of use. Pixar Entertainment is nearly synonymous with great animation and colorful characters. Hear the words "TED Talks" and you are probably reminded of thought-provoking speeches.

Brands shape the way we think. Brands are powerful. Teachers can harness that power. With a little thought, you can develop a brand identity for your classroom that can drive students to work harder, achieve more, and enjoy school more.

I can boil my five-part philosophy into the brand statement in the box below.

When I first developed this brand statement, it felt just right. The brand was exactly what I wanted my students to think when they thought about my classroom. In fact, I felt that I had already established that brand and that it was evident in the work I do with kids.

To make sure this was actually the message I was projecting, I surveyed the students by simply asking a random sampling to finish the sentence, In Mrs. Platt's

> *In Mrs. Platt's classroom we work hard, we have fun, and we learn.*

classes we . . . I was thrilled to find that the students agreed with my brand statement! Below are some of the responses I got.

In Mrs. Platt's classes we

- *have fun and enjoy ourselves while we work.*
- *work hard, have fun, and become more intelligent.*
- *know our hard work pays off.*
- *are hardworking and successful learners.*
- *are hardworking, mature, independent, responsible, and successful!*

Continually incorporate your brand into your classroom talk. Make it a part of your daily interactions. Refer to it in classroom discussions. Use it as a platform to discuss why you do things as you do.

In my class, I might start a lesson by saying, "Today we're going to read an article on the rock cycle. It's a challenging text, but I know you'll all do fine because you always work so hard to learn! The article is super interesting, so it'll be fun to read."

Last, share your brand widely! Put your brand statement on your webpage or school Facebook account, add it as a running head on assignments you hand out, and include it in rubrics to assess those assignments. Sometimes, the mere act of communicating the brand for your classroom goes a long way toward making it a reality.

### Joy and Effort, BFFs!

I hope this chapter has convinced you that student effort and joy go hand in hand in the most effective classrooms. The chapters to come all continue to support the connection between happy and hardworking classrooms.

---

#### Recapping the BIG Idea

***Joy and hard work go hand in hand in a teacher's efforts to motivate students to meet learning goals.***

**In this chapter we looked at:**

1. How joy matters to learning.
2. The connection between working hard and joy.
3. The role of self-control in a joyful classroom.
4. Rigor and the Gradual Release of Responsibility Model.
5. The three drivers of self-motivated learning.
6. Strategies, such as branding, to help you increase motivation, hard work, and joy in your classroom.

## References

Blackburn, B. (2017). *Four myths about rigor in the classroom.* Retrieved from www.middleweb.com/34738/four-myths-about-rigor-in-the-classroom/

Burns, M. (2012). *Dopamine and learning: What the Brain's reward center can teach educators.* Retrieved from www.scilearn.com/blog/dopamine-learning-brains-reward-center-teach-educators

Calarco, J. M. (2018). *Why rich kids are so good at the marshmallow test.* Retrieved from www.theatlantic.com/family/archive/2018/06/marshmallow-test/561779/

Dweck, C. S. (2017). *Mindset.* London: Robinson, an imprint of Constable & Robinson Ltd.

Edwards, S. (2010). Humor, laughter, and those aha moments. *On the Brain, 17*(2), 1–3. Retrieved from https://hms.harvard.edu/sites/default/files/HMS_OTB_Spring10_Vol16_No2.pdf

Fisher, D., & Frey, N. (2014). *Better learning through structured teaching: A framework for the gradual release of responsibility*, 2nd Edition. Alexandria, VA: Association for Supervision and Curriculum Development.

Fisher, M. (2016). *Hacking the common core: 10 strategies for amazing learning in a standardized world.* Cleveland, OH: X10 Publications.

Krashen, S. D. (1995). *Principles and practice in second language acquisition.* New York: Phoenix ELT.

Mischel, W. (2015). *The marshmallow test: Mastering self-control.* New York: Little, Brown and Company.

Pink, D. H. (2012). *Drive: The surprising truth about what motivates us.* New York: Riverhead Books.

Rankin, J. G. (2017). *First aid for teacher burnout: How you can find peace and success.* New York: Routledge.

Routman, R. (2018). *Literacy essentials: Engagement, excellence, and equity for all learners.* Portland, ME: Stenhouse.

Stambor, Z. (2006). How laughing leads to learning. *APA Monitor on Psychology, 37*(6), 62.

# 3

# Where Everyone Knows Your Name

> **The BIG Idea**
> *A positive school/classroom climate based on relationships is essential for learning.*
>
> **In this chapter you will:**
> 1. Define *climate* as it relates to classrooms and schools as a whole.
> 2. Read about why building relationships is the bottom line in effective classrooms.
> 3. Find strategies to help you build strong relationships with students.
> 4. Reflect on methods to develop and maintain a safe classroom for all learners through strong classroom management.
> 5. Learn what to do if your classroom is "out of control."

Happy classrooms, where all students are willing to take risks and challenge themselves to work hard and learn, begin with a foundation of strong relationships between all stakeholders. Teachers and students must know and respect each other, and that must also be true among students themselves. Building relationships is the secret of classroom management and helps promote a culture of caring and kindness. Classrooms where students feel safe and respected are positive places to be. They have good "climates."

## What is School or Classroom Climate?

In a few words, climate can be defined as the feel or tone of the school or classroom. In Chapter 2, you read about the importance of a joyful learning environment as it relates to student achievement. Classrooms that have positive climates are welcoming places where students feel safe, cared about, challenged, and for the most part, happy.

Another way to think about climate is in terms of the best-case scenario. In the best of all worlds, a class or school with a positive climate can be described as a "Bam!" classroom or school. Principal Baruti K. Kafele (2016), who coined the term, puts it this way, "A 'Bam!' classroom is one that provides students with an overwhelmingly magical and memorable experience" (p. 21).

While many of us don't have Bam! climates, that should certainly be the goal. The bottom line is that our students learn better in classrooms and schools with strong positive climates, and building relationships is central to getting there.

For another way to think about climate, look at the positive climate indicator list below.

- ✓ Students and teacher seem happy.
- ✓ Students and teacher work hard.
- ✓ All stakeholders are afforded respect.
- ✓ There are few behavior issues.
- ✓ Students freely contribute to classroom discussions.
- ✓ Students ask for needed help.
- ✓ Students report liking the teacher.

## The Theory and Research

This chapter is called "Where Everyone Knows Your Name." That is because a good classroom climate begins with good relationships. Before we move too deeply into strategies to help students feel like they are in a place where "everybody knows their name," let's consider the research on student-teacher relationships and on positive classroom climate.

### It is All About Relationships

Read the quotes on p. 34 and think about how they relate to your beliefs about school and classroom climate.

**Your Turn!**

★ Think about the climate in your school and/or classroom. Use the chart below to help you reflect on strengths and potential areas for improvement.

| Indicator | I am *confident* this is true. | I *think* this is *probably* true. | This is *not* true or I don't know if it's true. |
|---|---|---|---|
| My students are happy to come to class most days. | | | |
| My students know I care about them. | | | |
| Students treat other students and me with respect. | | | |
| My students work hard most of the time. | | | |
| There are few behavior issues in my classroom. | | | |
| My students think of me as a good teacher. | | | |
| I have strong relationships with my students. I know them. They know me. | | | |

★ Reflect on the areas where you feel you could improve.
★ Think back to the section on branding in Chapter 2. Can you see a relationship between classroom branding and climate?
★ Formulate a "SMART" goal to help you make needed changes.

1. *Students don't care how much you know until they know how much you care.*
   – Anonymous

2. *School climate isn't another thing on the plate – it is the plate!*
   – Peter Dewitt (ASCD, 2017)

3. *They may forget what you said, but they will never forget how you made them feel.*
   –Carl W. Buechner (Evans, 1971)

4. *It is teachers who have created positive teacher-student relationships that are more likely to have the above average effects on student achievement.*
   – John Hattie (Australian Society for Evidence Based Teaching, 2018)

> **Meta-analysis**
>
> a statistical analysis of several separate but similar experiments or studies in order to test the pooled data for statistical significance
>
> – Merriam-Webster

Below you will see a chart taken from *Visible Learning* a book written by education researcher John Hattie (2009) drives home just how important relationships are. Hattie does meta-analyses of meta-analyses. While that might initially sound like gobbledygook, the worst type of edu-babble, it is actually a simple concept. To understand what Hattie does, first we need to define the term "meta-analysis." A meta-analysis is what happens when researchers look at multiple studies on a given topic and aggregate the data to derive a single set of results. For example, if a researcher wanted to know how effective a strategy is – let's say, students understanding learning targets – the researcher looks at all of the available studies on students' knowledge of learning targets. The researcher uses a statistical approach to combine the data from all of the studies in order to obtain an effect strength. Got it so far? Now, what is an "effect strength"? It is, in very simple terms, the probable impact a given strategy will have.

Now, take all that you read above and consider what John Hattie does. Hattie takes established educational meta-analyses and meta-analyzes them! In his book *Visible Learning* (2009), Hattie synthesized over 800 meta-analyses of educational research to share a list of the 139 influences on student academic achievement. Each influence on the list is ranked by effect strength, or amount of impact. If an influence is ranked as having an effect strength of .4 or higher, it is an influence that should be taken very seriously by educators who wish to improve student achievement outcomes. The results of Hattie's work is interesting and sometimes very surprising, and I highly recommend teachers read one of Hattie's books (there's also *Visible Learning for Teachers*) or google his latest list of effect strengths.

Hattie's analysis of the research finds that there is a very high positive impact on students' learning when there is a strong teacher–student relationship. The effect strength is approximately .74! Remember, the tipping point for impact is only .4. It is abundantly clear that building teacher-student relationships is a critical best practice!

### Simple Tips, Hints, and Ideas to Foster Positive Relationships

Students who know and feel known by their teachers are more likely to work hard, behave well, and be open to new ideas. Similarly, families who feel connected to the school are more likely to support the school's mission and their children's teachers. So, in every conceivable way, it behooves teachers to make building relationships central to their work. Below are several simple tips, hints, and ideas to help you foster positive teacher-student relationships.

1. Have some low-key fun!

    Set up a meetup or two. Meetups are easy to plan for and fun. They are as simple as putting out an invitation to folks to meet you at a chosen location. In June and July, for example, I often post messages on Facebook, like the examples below.

    *Hey SCF Peeps! I'll be at the SCF Public Library on Friday from 4:00–6:30 just hoping some of my students and families will stop by and hang out with me! Let's chat, check out books, and have a little fun! See you then!*

    *Friday night! Music on the Overlook! Be there or be square! Hoping to see lots of Saints dancing the night way. (FYI: I teach in St. Croix Falls and we are the SCF "Saints.")*

2. Flip the fun on Flipgrid!

    If you haven't tried Flipgrid (https://flipgrid.com/) yet, you must! Here is how the website describes its free product,

    > Flipgrid is where your students go to share ideas and learn together. It's where students amplify and feel amplified. It's video the way students use video. Short. Authentic. And fun! That's why it's the leading video discussion platform used by tens of millions of PreK to PhD educators, students, and families.

Make a free account and try using it to stay connected to your students. I promise you, it is incredibly easy. Users click a huge green plus sign to add a video and a huge talking bubble to respond to another user. After you get your account, follow the steps below.
The topics for chat are endless. Ask about what your students are reading, how their jobs are going, the funniest thing that has happened to them, where they are going on vacation, how much they love you, anything!

– Make a new "grid" and call it "How's it going?" "Tell me about your goals" "What's your favorite song?" or anything else you want to ask.
– Record a video of yourself.
– Give students and families the URL and code for your grid.
– Watch the magic happen!

> **Grid Name**: EduQuotes for EduGeeks
> **URL**: https://flipgrid.com/fe0786
> **Password**: Joy&Effort

I made a grid for readers of this book so you can see how it works and we can get to know each other! Go to the URL in the box and use the password provided. Then, tell me about your favorite education-related quote and I'll chat back with you! You will be amazed at how easy and fun it is to use!

3  **Conduct interest inventories**

An interest inventory is a simple worksheet where your students can share information about themselves with teachers. The inventory can take many forms. It can consist of a few questions or dozens, opportunities for free-form writing, or questions/statements with Likert scales. They are easy to find on the internet. I did a simple Google search using the term "interest inventory students" and came up with dozens of good examples. Read the scenario below to see how one teacher uses interest inventories to connect with her students.

*Ms. Schnieder (not her real name) teaches fifth grade at an urban middle school. She uses interest inventories several times each school year to get a feel for her students as people.*

*"I like to ask my kids questions that can help me know them deeply as individuals. I want to know what they like in school, what their hopes and dreams are, and maybe, most importantly, what they like to do outside of school. I change the questions often but I always include something about what they want to be when they grow up, what type of music they like, what sports they play, what*

*pets they have, and what they like in a friend. I think the answers to those questions are really helpful for me as I build relationships with my students.*

*"After I read the surveys, I jot down key information on my seating chart. I note what career each kid is interested in and what genre of music they prefer. Then, I refer to those things often. For example, I might have hiphop music playing when students come to class on Monday morning and I'll say, 'Hey, Tiawana and Javon! Did you notice I'm playing your music today?' Then the next day, I'll play country music and give a shout-out to the students who prefer that genre.*

*"Where I really focus, though, is on students' hopes for their futures. If we're doing geometry and I know that a student wants to become an architect or a construction foreman like her uncle, I'll say, 'Tommy and Rochelle, this is going to be really important information for you two because you'll use a ton of geometry in your work as an architect and construction.' Or, if we're reading poetry, I might say, 'Abdul! You're going to love reading this poem! It'll give you a chance to practice your actor voice and move you closer to being a movie star!' Honestly, I think that little efforts like this go a long way to helping my kids realize how much I care about them."*

### 4  Keep culture in mind

Schools can be a great place to experience the wonderful diversity of communities. In order to keep classrooms humming with positive and productive energy, it is incumbent on teachers to get to know the cultures of our students. Scholar Gloria Ladson-Billings (2009) coined the term "culturally relevant pedagogy." Loosely defined, it means ensuring that what and how you teach meets a student's cultural needs and understandings. Ladsen-Billings delved into research focusing on why some teachers were more effective teaching African American students than were others,

> *The study revealed that teachers who were most effective in communicating with the students used an interactional style that the authors termed 'culturally congruent' . . . which was meant to signify the ways in which teachers altered their speech patterns, communication styles, and participation structures to resemble more closely those of the students' own culture.*
>
> (p. 18)

This means that we must learn, read, ask questions, and generally get to know as much as we can about the cultures of the children we teach. My own experiences in the classroom have included many cross-cultural experiences that have taught me to take the time to learn about the cultures of the students I serve and to listen to their verbal and nonverbal cues about what works best for them as learners. Read the story below as an example. Then, ask yourself how you can get to know the cultures of the students you teach.

*In my second year teaching, I embarked on a big adventure. I lived in Alaska and left the comfort of the road system to teach in a remote, fly-in access Inuit village on the coast of the Bering Sea. The village, Stebbins, was home to less than 500 people, all of whom had been born and raised in Inuit culture. I taught first and second grade in the village school and quickly fell in love with the place and the people. But, I was young and not as informed as I could have been. I knew little of the history and culture of the Inuit children I served.*

*One day, I caught little Irwin doing something naughty. I have long since forgotten what. I scolded Irwin and he stood facing me, hands clasped, and eyes cast downward. Once I was finished lecturing, I said, "Do you understand me, Irwin?" He didn't respond. So, I said it again, "Irwin, do you understand me?" Still no response. I was getting angry and I said, "Irwin!" this time quite loudly, "Answer me! Do you understand?" When Irwin still didn't respond I sent him to the time-out chair and he sat sadly watching the other kids go outside for recess.*

*Later, that day, I debriefed the experience with another teacher. This woman, Mrs. Trevithick, had been teaching in the village for several years. When I told her what happened she said, "Oh dear. Was Irwin lifting his eyebrows up and down?" When I acknowledged that I had seen that and wondered what he was doing, Mrs. Trevithick taught me a valuable lesson in cross-cultural communication. "Rita," she said, "In Inuit culture, raising the eyebrows is the same as saying, yes. Irwin was responding! You better find him and apologize!"*

## Building a Safe Climate of Caring and Achievement

Teachers and students must have strong relationships, but that doesn't mean that teachers and students should be BFFs! The teacher can be friendly, warm, empathetic, and caring and still hold students accountable to excellent work

**Your Turn!**
- ★ Take some time to surf the web for good interest inventories.
- ★ Choose questions to use or modify, or design your own questions.
- ★ Think about how you can use the answers you get from students to help them feel you know and care about them.

and behavior. Truly, if we want positive classroom climates, then having a safe and well-run classroom is essential.

Take a look at the guidelines for strong and productive student-teacher relationships below, which were adapted from the *Australian Society for Evidence Based Teaching (2018)*.

As a part of a healthy teacher-student relationship, children need to understand that

- they must adhere to the routines, procedures, expectations, and rules of the classroom.
- they can and should behave well.
- they can and should work hard to learn.
- their teachers will provide guidance and structure they can depend on.
- they will get the academic and social support they need to meet school/classroom standards.

### Safety in Routines and Management

Having strong routines and management plans in place for students can help keep your classroom humming with productivity and can stave off misunderstandings and even conflicts.

Routines

For the purposes of this book, routines can be defined as the procedures and systems in place for accomplishing the day-to-day business of the classroom. Examples of questions that can be answered with routines are listed below.

- How should students enter or leave a classroom?
- What should students do upon arrival?
- What material do students need to have on their desks?
- How do students ask for help?
- What should students do if they were or are going to be absent?
- What should students do if they need to use the restroom or get a drink of water?
- How should work be turned in and papers be passed out?
- How and when should students use electronic devices?

Never underestimate the power of direct instruction, modeling, and reteaching routines. In my experience, the most successful, least stressed, and often happiest teachers have strong systems in place that are explicitly taught, frequently modeled, and reviewed as needed. Similarly, students are likely to work harder and feel more relaxed and happy when they know what is expected of them. Take a look at a few examples below.

1. *And so it begins!* Do your students know how they are expected to come into the room and what they should do when they get there? If they don't or if teachers don't hold them accountable to the routines, time is going to be wasted. Most teachers agree – there is no time to waste! This is especially true in grades where students move to different rooms for each class. Many classes are only 40 minutes long. Losing a couple of minutes at arrival and dismissal, say four minutes a day, might not sound like much until you do the math and realize that it is 10% of weekly class time! Students need to enter the room, get busy, and work productively until the end of class. To make that happen, teachers use a variety of strategies. One that is currently sweeping the education nation is the "Do Now" concept.

    *Do Now* is a strategy from the fantastic book, *Teach Like a Champion* (Lemov, 2010, p. 152). In a nutshell, the teacher chooses a spot on the whiteboard, chalkboard, or interactive smart board to post a task for students to complete immediately as they enter the classroom; in other words, they are to "do it now." It must be a task that is possible for all students to complete independently and within a few minutes. The *Do Now* can take countless forms. Examples include a question or problem of the day, a short text for students to read, a reminder to review notes, or even quiet study with a partner. Whatever you chose to use, it should focus on current, past, or even future learning targets.

2. *Come together!* Having routines for getting students' attention is also important. What signal will you use when you want all eyes on you? It could be a bell, chime, or even a duck call as a teacher friend of mine uses, which brings plenty of laughter to her colleagues! You might choose to use a phrase – "May I please have your attention" works well. So does a call and response, for example, when the teacher says, "Class! Class!" the students follow with, "Yes? Yes?" Personally, I always use the countdown method. I loudly call, "Five!" and then more quietly countdown from four to one to give students a chance to finish their thoughts or sentences.

    No matter what signal you use, don't forget that you have to teach and model it. Do not expect students to know how to actively listen. Show them what you mean when you ask for attention. Teach them to look at you, be still, listen, and think about what you are saying. Then, of course, make sure they do just that. Never continue to talk above the voices of your students. If you do, they will quickly learn that they do not have to listen to you.

3. *You're NEVER "done"!* What teacher hasn't seen a student sitting at their desk doing nothing, claiming to be "done"? Done? With learning? Never! Students must know the procedures for continuing to learn when they are finished with a discrete assignment. Having a list of "things to do when you are done" that students can quickly access can be incredibly helpful. Some teachers make a *What to Do When I'm Done* "anchor chart" (a poster that remains up as an anchor to learning and that the teacher and students refer to frequently). Or have a basket of content-related worksheets or short articles that students can engage with when they are done with the work you've assigned. Look at the example provided and think about how you could make an anchor chart that fits the needs of your classroom.

Image 3.1 "What to do when you're done" anchor chart.

4. *Hello again! Glad to see you!* What will students do if they are absent? When I taught in a large junior high school, as I took roll and noted an absent student, I assigned her/him a "buddy." The buddy took

two copies of all papers passed out, made a copy of her/his notes, and made a plan to share the information with the absent student when she or he returned. This method was not only good for the absent student, but it also promoted a team connection in the class and helped to build ownership for learning. Other teachers keep a file for each class they teach with sections for each day of the week. As they pass out material or assignments, they put an extra copy into the file. Those teachers who use online platforms such as Google Classroom or Schoology simply post all assignments, readings, handouts, and notes online for easy access. They then teach students that when they return from an absence, it is their responsibility to find what they missed and make an appointment to meet with you if they need help.

5  *Help me! Please?* Teaching students to ask for help is a gift we can give them. Below, you will read about how character education connects to classroom climates that are happy and hardworking. One positive character trait that is often overlooked is *assertion*. I teach students that being *assertive* means having the strength to ask for what you want or need, or helping others do the same, with thoughtfulness and a positive tone. Having systems in place so that students can ask for help when needed teaches positive assertion. Whatever system you chose, be sure to talk with students about how they know they need help before asking for it. A teacher friend of mine hung paper shopping bags from her ceiling, each with "Fight your way out of a paper bag!" written on all sides in black sharpie. She had grown frustrated by students asking for help before they took the time to reflect on whether they could solve a problem independently. I asked the teacher, Mrs. Scott, about it and she said,

– *I had kids asking me what page to work on when it was written on the board. Or asking me if they had to write in cursive, even though we always write in cursive. Of course, I'm happy to help, I mean, I teach because I like helping kids, but I felt like I was not teaching them to be independent. So, I told them a story about a kid who was trapped inside a paper bag and just couldn't get out. I asked them what the kid should do. Most immediately said the kids should rip his way out.*
– *I used that as a teaching point to tell them that they too could 'Fight their way out of a paper bag and figure some things out without just jumping to asking me to help them.' It really did work! It was helpful!*

When students really do need help, try using "Ask three before me." That means that students who need help should ask three peers before they ask the teacher. If none of their peers know the answer, then it is time to seek adult help. This simple strategy also works

Image 3.2 "Fight your way out of a paper bag" teaching tip.

to help students make supportive connections with one another. If independent work is required or a quiet room is important, try colored cards. Give students an index card with a red dot on one side and a green dot on the other. If all is well, the student leaves the green side facing up. If he or she needs help, the card is flipped to the red side. This requires that teachers are up and circulating the classroom while students work.

> **Your Turn!**
> - ★ Jot down a list of possible teaching points to make your classroom feel safe and comfortable for students.
> - ★ Think about the routines that may need to be explicitly taught.
> - ★ Plan for time to intentionally reteach routines. Mark the days you'll return to each routine on your calendar so you don't forget.

## Management

Related to the information and strategies you are about to learn, *management* will refer to the systems in place for helping students understand desired behaviors as well as the consequences for not exhibiting those desired behaviors. Perhaps most importantly, management includes learning to be proactive about helping students remain hardworking and happy.

### Starting with clear rules and consequences for not respecting them

A well-organized classroom where students know, understand, and follow established routines and procedures is much more likely to promote a positive climate than classrooms characterized by disorganization or unclear expectations. If your rules aren't clear or easily followed, your students may have a hard time conforming to them.

The best classroom rules follow three guidelines:

1. Limit the number to a maximum of five basic rules.
2. Positively state all rules.
3. Allow students to participate in making or defining the rules. Look at the samples below and notice how simply and positively stated they are.

| Rules Sample 1 | Rules Sample 2 | Rules Sample 3 |
|---|---|---|
| Respect others. | Be on time. | Be cooperative. |
| Be helpful. | Be prepared. | Try hard. |
| Follow directions. | Be respectful. | Be kind. |
| Ask questions. | Work hard. | |
| Work hard. | | |

Some teachers ask students to be part of the rule-developing process and that is, of course, fine. But it is not totally necessary, either. Students can have a voice in classroom rules even if they are created exclusively by the teacher. Think back to the "looks like, sounds like, feels like" you completed in Chapter 1. Once your established rules have been communicated to students, involve the class in a "looks like, sounds like, feels like" activity to help them think about and internalize what the rules mean. Ask students to brainstorm what each rule might look like, sound like, and feel like if enacted in the classroom. This activity should be teacher-led so that you can guide students through the discussion about the rules and the charts. See the examples below for clarification.

| What does being *prepared* mean? | | |
|---|---|---|
| **Looks Like** | **Sounds Like** | **Feels Like** |
| • Have a pencil<br>• Have my textbook<br>• Did my homework | • Quiet work<br>• Not whispering to borrow materials | • Stress free!<br>• Comfortable<br>• Productive |

| What does *working hard* mean? | | |
|---|---|---|
| **Looks Like** | **Sounds Like** | **Feels Like** |
| • Students engaged<br>• Head bent over desks<br>• Students writing or making something | • Quiet talking sometimes<br>• Silence sometimes<br>• Asking questions | • Challenging<br>• Learning<br>• Productive<br>• Pride in myself |

## Consequences

Once you have established clear rules and elaborated on them with examples, as illustrated in the charts above, you will need to develop and share consequences that will be applied when students do not follow them. Safe classrooms must have clearly defined and progressive consequences in place for when a student does not follow the rules.

Consequences can be simple and tailored to the needs of a given classroom. Below is a list of the progressive consequences in an eighth grade math classroom.

1. Warning
2. Short detention with discussion
3. Written plan for improvement

4  Parent or guardian contact
5  Initiate principal involvement

Another list comes from a fifth grade classroom.

1  Teacher will give you a verbal reminder.
2  You will take a time-out to think about how to follow the rules.
3  You will write a letter to your parents or guardian telling them about what happened.
4  Teacher will write a referral for you to see the principal.

Progressive consequences are most effective when they are clear and consistent, posted, discussed with students, and shared with parents.

**Being Proactive**

Rules and consequences are an important part of developing a strong positive classroom climate. However, it might even be more important that teachers understand the "whats" and "whys" behind a given student's behavior. For the most part, when students misbehave, they are trying to fulfill a need. There is a reason for the misbehavior; this is often referred to as the "function of the behavior." When teachers can identify the function of the behavior, they can proactively meet a student's needs before a problem arises.

In her wonderful book *Cooperative Discipline*, Linda Albert (2003) shared the four most common functions of behavior as the need for attention, power, revenge, and avoidance of failure. Knowing these functions and learning to recognize them can help teachers keep students working hard and feeling happy. On the following page is a description of each of the four main functions of behavior with both the associated misbehaviors that can help you identify them and suggestions to proactively meet students' needs.

---

**Your Turn!**
- ★ Reflect on rules and consequences in your classroom and decide if they are well aligned with the best practices shared above.
- ★ If not, decide on changes that will help you make your classroom feel safe for students.
- ★ Try doing a "looks like, sounds like, feels like" chart with your students for one or more of your classroom rules.

### The four main functions of behavior

1. *Attention*: Students whose main function of behavior is getting attention will work hard to get it any way they can, including by misbehaving, because even negative attention is better than no attention at all. When students crave attention, you might see them exhibiting the following behaviors.
   - Tapping pencil on desk
   - Making noise
   - Often out of seat
   - Calling out answers
   - Interrupting
   - Asking irrelevant questions

   Once you identify this need, try to limit the attention you give to inappropriate behavior, and focus instead on positive behaviors and on the student's achievements. Giving the student positive attention when appropriate will help them to see that they can receive the attention they crave and that it feels better when it is positive rather than negative. Possible ways to give students the attention they need proactively are included on the list below.
   - Pat the student on the shoulder from time to time.
   - Make frequent eye contact and smile at the student often.
   - Call on the student in class (when you are sure that he or she knows the answer!).
   - Pass the student a note with a cheerful comment, specific praise, or compliment.
   - Give brief, specific praise about the student's work or behavior.
   - Converse briefly with the student before and after class.
   - Select the student to carry out a task or be a regular helper.
   - Make frequent positive phone calls home.

2. *Avoidance of failure*: Students who have avoidance of failure as their main function of behavior are scared that they will not be successful. Students with avoidance of failure can be those who typically struggle academically or who are behind national academic norms. These students have not had a taste of success and come to expect they might never have one in the future either. The converse can be true as well. Students who are typically thought of as high achievers may have never "failed" before and don't want to start now! When students have a fear of failure, you might see one or more of the following behaviors.
   - Stops working.
   - Procrastinates.

- Becomes easily frustrated.
- Shuts down.
- Does work that is below ability.
- Cries.
- Puts head down on desk.

For these students, it is important to "chunk" work into smaller steps. Instead of giving them the entire assignment, give them one piece at a time so that they can experience mini-successes as they finish each. It is also beneficial for these students to learn that "failure" is a perfectly normal part of the learning process. Modeling your own mistakes and celebrating growth, progress, or effort are also helpful. Remember what you read in Chapter 1 about flipping failure on its head by teaching that failure is often a part of eventual success. Remind your students to think of FAIL as an acronym that stands for First Attempt In Learning. Try these ways to proactively support students who have a fear of failure are listed below.

- Chunk work – for example, do not give the entire worksheet, give sections of it or five math problems at a time.
- Praise *effort*, not *success* – "I like how hard you're working!" or "It is great to see you digging into your work like that! Let me know if you have questions." Rather than, "You are smart!" or "Awesome! You got an A!"
- Ask student to help others.
- Work with student to set manageable goals.

3. *Revenge*: Students who seek revenge are, unfortunately, both those who push a teacher's buttons the most and those that are the most difficult to proactively help. Students whose main function of behavior is to take revenge often have been mistreated for a long period of time at home or at school. These students often come across as angry or disaffected. They can be noncompliant and downright mean in addition to the misbehaviors listed below.
   - Sullen
   - Withdrawn
   - Rude to teacher and classmates
   - Extremely angry
   - Resorting to violent behavior

To help these students, teachers often need to seek outside help from counselors or social workers. A key with students whose need is to get revenge is to stay calm and remember to put your ego aside. These students are seeking the help they need, and it is better for them and for the teacher if the teacher can learn to take a breath and not take the student's behavior personally. No matter what is happening, try to focus on love. That might sound hippy-dippy, but when we remind ourselves that we are the stewards of our fellow human beings, it becomes easier to accept the behaviors they display, and we can encourage ourselves to dislike the behavior but not the person. Steps that can be taken in the classroom are to let the student know that you care about her or him despite their behavior choices. Do this by letting the student know that it is not him/her that you disapprove of or are unhappy with, it is the behavior. You can also teach them to watch for warning signs of inappropriate behavior, or triggers, in themselves and work with the student to determine skills or actions that can be taken to settle themselves down and/or to avoid the behavior. Here are proactive measures a teacher can take are listed below.

- Explicitly teach students to recognize feelings and to express them.
- Teach students to look for triggers to their anger and then to avoid them.
- Teach students self-calming strategies, including deep breathing and slowly counting backward from ten to one.
- Ask for help from another adult – sometimes there are students who are more comfortable with other adults who can offer help, rather than with their own classroom teacher.

4 *Power*: Students who are angling for power can be of two types. First, and most obvious, are the ones who seem to want to take over the class and teach it themselves! But you might be surprised to learn that the students who are noncompliant and just quietly refuse to do the work you assign are very often also seeking power. Students in need of power just want to feel they have voice and choice. When students seek power, you might see any of the following behaviors.

- Tantrums/yelling
- Talking back
- Refusal to obey
- Saying things similar to "You can't make me do it!"
- Folded arms and a defiant expression

As misbehavior types go, power is a relatively easy one to proactively prevent. The key is to give students choices and to allow them to share their opinions and ideas for the class. One way to do that is to give students options in assignments. In the chapter on differentiated instruction, you will be presented with many ideas for modifying assignments so students meet

the same learning targets but in different ways. Other ways to offer students power are by having a student suggestion box and giving students surveys to solicit their feedback (more on this in Chapter 5). The more students see that you value their input, the more power they feel they have. If you do have students who exhibit a need for power, the following suggestions should prove helpful.
- Give the student two options to choose from based on the behavior you expect.
- Ask for and use feedback from students about day-to-day life in your classroom and/or school (more information on this in Chapter 5).

Using Albert's model for understanding and proactively addressing behavior concerns has been a very helpful tool for many teachers. Of course, it is important to remember that children, like adults, are complex. Use the information above as a guide, not as a way to label students or pigeonhole their needs.

**Simple Tips, Hints, and Ideas for Managing a Classroom**
There are many great tools available to help teachers work on developing a classroom management plan that works to maintain a happy and industrious classroom environment. Read through the suggestions below and maybe even try a few out!

1 Use technology tools
*Class DoJo* (www.classdojo.com/) is a free behavior tracking app or website that allows teachers to track good and bad behavior choices. Each student gets her or his own avatar and can participate in earning points. Teachers can award students points and badges for everything from turning work in on time to helping fellow students. Points can also be subtracted. The data is stored and can be used in conferring with students, parents, and other educators as needed. Users claim that its game-like format is engaging and motivating and that students love it. One of the best parts of Class DoJo is that it helps teachers and students see successes rather than focusing on negatives. It takes minutes to set up your class.

*TooLoud?* (https://itunes.apple.com/us/app/tooloud-pro/id425137981?mt=8) and *Too Noisy* (http://toonoisyapp.com/) are apps that allow teachers to set an acceptable noise level for a given activity. Then a phone or tablet can be used as a listening device. If the students get too loud, an alarm sounds.

2  **The character education connection**
If we want students to show good character, it helps to model good character and provide students with many examples. No matter what content you teach, there are likely examples of professionals in the field who exhibit positive character traits that if students were to emulate would lead to a safe and more productive classroom. In English language arts, there are countless authors with strong positive character traits. Of course that is also true of artists, athletes, and musicians. Social studies teachers will, of course, easily find examples of cooperative, caring, hardworking, and helpful people to share with students. Harness the power of these examples by pointing them out to students. Try making a simple poster like the one below, which might be used in an art classroom.

3  **Go visiting!**
Never let your ego get in the way of improving your practice. No matter how good any of us are as teachers, we have plenty to learn from our colleagues. Ask your students or your principal what teachers have particularly strong classroom management, including routines and procedures in their classroom. Chat with those teachers about why they think they are so successful, and ask if you can visit their classrooms to see their classroom management strategies in action.

---

### KEITH HARING IS A PERSON OF CHARACTER!

Keith Haring is <u>giving</u> and <u>helpful</u>

- He donated time and money to help people fighting AIDS.
- He opened a "PopShop" to make his art available to more than just rich art dealers.
- He started a foundation that offered low-cost art-making workshops to children and funded AIDS research.
- He was an activist for gay rights.

"You have to be objective about money to use it fairly. It doesn't make you any better or any more useful than any other person. Even if you use your money to help people, that doesn't make you better than somebody who has no money but is sympathetic and genuinely loving to fellow human beings." (Haring, 2010)

Figure 3.1  Embedded character education.

4  **Assume best intentions!**
   See your students' better angels. Sometimes we think a student is being disrespectful and later realize that it was not at all their intention. "Killing them with kindness" and "You catch more flies with honey than vinegar" are hackneyed sayings, at least in part, because they speak to a deep truth. Respond to students as if they intend to work hard and meet your expectations. You might be surprised at how often they rise to meet your expectations! Of course, they won't always. They are kids, and sometimes there will be undesirable behaviors. If you feel a student is being rude or otherwise disrespectful, confront her/him with care. The key is to not let your emotions or ego rule your response. Wait until you're calm and then try saying in a relaxed, kind tone, "You may not have meant to be rude but when you _____, it made me feel _____. Can we talk about it?"

## What if Your Classroom is "Out of Control"?

I hope that the information above has helped you to see the connection between keeping a classroom running smoothly and maintaining classroom culture of joy and effort. Strong classroom management is the bottom line in effective teaching. A classroom that is "in control" is one where students are focused and learning occurs.

However, it is important to remember that a loud or active classroom does not necessarily equal one that is out of control. Joy is essential to learning, and sometimes joy means a bit of controlled chaos, right? There is no need to be dogmatic about what style of classroom management is best or exactly what the just right amount of noise or movement is. There are as many effective methods to keep a class productively humming as there are teachers at the helms of classes. There are, however, some common look-fors to determine if a class is out of control and in need of a turnaround. Check your responses to the questions below.

| In my classroom: | Yes | No |
| --- | --- | --- |
| Am I happy and relaxed? | | |
| Are my students happy and relaxed? | | |
| Is learning the focus? | | |
| Do students make demonstrable growth in the content I teach? | | |

If you answered "no" to one or more of the questions, your classroom might be out of control and you may need to push the reset button. If so, there are four big-picture priorities to improve upon. Ask yourself these questions.

| Do I consistently: | Yes | No |
|---|---|---|
| Ensure that expectations and routines are clear? | | |
| Cultivate strong mutually respectful relationships? | | |
| Provide differentiation and meaningful work? | | |
| Celebrate student success? | | |

If you answered "no" one or more times, it's probably time for a focused effort to learn how to change your classroom such that you can answer "yes," because unless the four elements above are in place, management or keeping kids "in control" will be a constant challenge.

Sometimes, even when you can answer "yes" to both sets of questions, a class can become hard to manage. When that happens, call on students to reflect on their behavior and set goals to make positive changes. Several years ago, I taught seventh grade English language arts and had an out-of-control class. The group was inclusive of six students who had Individual Education Plans (IEPs) for behavior disorders.

The class was having difficulty working independently during their silent reading time, and students were increasingly off task and silly. I had come to love the group and was sure that with a little effort we could get back on track. I took steps to get the group working hard and happy again and the steps worked! Of course, I had to continue to tweak structures all year, but by and large, what you see below was my roadmap to success.

1. First I video recorded students as they worked on an assignment and during instruction. I did not ask them to make any changes. I wanted a video record of a regular day.
2. The next day, I told students that we were going to watch the video. I asked students to draw two "plus-minus"

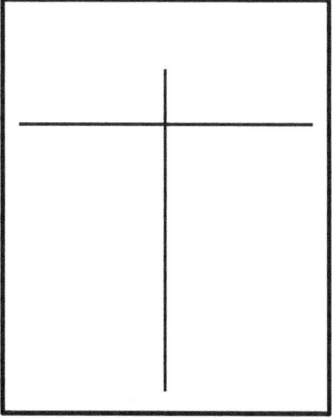

Figure 3.2 Blank "plus-minus" chart.

charts. The first labeled "What I Should See" and the second "What I Did See."

3. Before I played the tape, I led students in a brief discussion about class expectations. I asked, "How should students behave during a lesson or work session? How shouldn't they behave?" I modeled writing ideas for how students should behave in the plus side of the "What I Should See" chart and ideas for how they shouldn't behave in the minus side. I then allowed students to work together to brainstorm answers and fill in the rest of the chart. After a few minutes, we shared our thoughts as a whole group.

4. After the discussion, I showed students the video of themselves during class, asking them to notice and record positive and negative behaviors on the "What I Did See" chart. I reminded them to not use specific names and to be sure to claim their own behavior rather than pointing fingers at the behavior of classmates.

5. Once they had watched the video, I allowed for five minutes of silent reflection and led the class in three quick writes: One, "How can I improve as a student?"; two, "How can the entire class improve?"; and three, "How can Mrs. Platt improve or help us do better?"

6. We used the results to develop the rubric below to help students self-monitor their independent reading workshop time.

| 4: Excellent | 3: Sufficient | 2: Needs Work | 1: Poor Choices |
|---|---|---|---|
| • Got right to work<br>• Stayed on task<br>• Focused on goals<br>• Transitioned well<br>• Was respectful | • Got right to work<br>• Mostly on task<br>• Focused on goals<br>• Transitioned well<br>• Mostly respectful | • Needed a reminder to get to work or to stay on task<br>• Focused on reading but not on specific personal goals<br>• Not always respectful | • Wasted time<br>• Needed more than one reminder to stay on task<br>• Was disrespectful |

7. From then on, I had students review the rubric before each class and set a goal for a score they would work for during independent reading. At the end of class, I had students self-assess and I added their scores to the gradebook. If we disagreed on a score, I conferred with the student until we reached consensus. Occasionally, and without warning, I would also issue students a score.

> **Recapping the BIG Idea**
>
> *A positive school/classroom climate based on relationships is essential for learning.*
>
> **In this chapter we looked at:**
> 1. Climate as it relates to classrooms and schools as a whole.
> 2. Strategies to help you build strong relationships with students.
> 3. Student needs that sometimes underlie poor behavior and how to proactively work to meet your students' needs.
> 4. Routines that help ensure that your classroom is safe for all learners.

The strategy worked exceptionally well, and I have used it in modified form several times since! It promotes ownership and self-awareness. One thing to be very careful of, however, is not embarrassing students. I use the strategy with a good amount of humor and no scolding. I use it with a heart of love, focused on a more positive future for the class. Do not attempt the strategy if you are feeling angry, irritated, or resentful.

## References

Albert, L. (2003). *Cooperative discipline: Teachers handbook*. Circle Pines, MN: AGS Publications.

ASCD Live.Learn.Teach. Radio. (2017). *How safe and supportive is your school climate?* Retrieved from www.bamradionetwork.com/ascd-learn-teach-lead-radio/4251-how-safe-and-supportive-is-your-school-climate

Australian Society for Evidence Based Teaching. (2018). *Teacher student relationships crucial to results*. Retrieved from www.evidencebasedteaching.org.au/crash-course-evidence-based-teaching/teacher-student-relationships/

Evans, R. L. (1971). *"Spoken word" and "thought for the day" and from many inspiring thought-provoking sources from many centuries quote*. Quote Page 244, Column 2. Salt Lake City, Utah: Publishers Press.

Hattie, J. (2009). *Visible learning: A synthesis of over 800 meta-analyses relating to achievement*. London: Routledge.

Kafele, B. K. (2016). *The teacher 50: Critical questions for inspiring classroom excellence*. Alexandria, VA: ASCD.

Ladson-Billings, G. (2009). *The dreamkeepers: Successful teachers of African American children*, 2nd Edition. Hoboken, New Jersey: John Wiley & Sons.

Lemov, D. (2010). *Teach like a champion: 49 techniques that put students on the path to college*. San Francisco: Jossey-Bass.

# 4

# Mastery Matters!

> **The BIG Idea**
> 
> *When students realize they can master difficult content, they are more motivated and more joyful about learning.*
>
> **In this chapter you will:**
> 1. Connect the concept of mastery with increasing student effort and making learning more joyful.
> 2. Learn strategies to help students increase the quality of the work they do.
> 3. Discover how standards-based learning can help teachers teach less content but teach it better.
> 4. Read about strategies that can help students see themselves as capable of mastery and encourage them to do their best.

Motivation can hinge on students seeing themselves as capable of mastery. Once students learn to set and meet goals, they will begin to see themselves as successful and autonomous learners. Helping students see evidence of their own learning will make the classroom happier and more productive. This chapter will explore strategies to build students' abilities to master material and to help them see themselves making progress.

# Mastery Matters

## The Theory and Research

Before moving forward, let's take a peek backward. In Chapter 2, you read about Daniel Pink's research on motivation. If you recall, the three components that tend to be in place when people are motivated are autonomy, purpose, and mastery. While the definition of the term *mastery* is up for debate, for the purposes of this book, we will define it this way:

> **Mastery = Proven ability to perform a skill or strategy with accuracy, or to prove a given learning standard has been met.**

When students are motivated, they apply more effort and school is a wonderful place to be. So, what does mastery have to do with motivation? Think of it in two related ways.

1. *Visible learning*: Researcher John Hattie (2009) coined the term *visible learning* to represent students' awareness of their learning goals and their progress toward meeting them. When students know what they are supposed to be learning or how they should be progressing and then see themselves making progress and mastering content, *visible learning* happens and is very motivating!
2. *Success breeds success*: A little bit of success can be a powerful thing! When students see themselves achieving, making progress, meeting goals, and successfully mastering content, they begin to trust themselves as learners. They are more willing to take risks and put forth effort and thus, success follows success! Massachusetts Institute of Technology neuroscientist Earl Miller puts it this way,

*The pleasurable feeling that comes with the successes is brought about by a surge in the neurotransmitter dopamine. By telling brain cells when they have struck gold, the chemical apparently signals them to keep doing whatever they did that led to success.*

(Joelving, 2009)

If students are to be motivated by mastery, there are certain premises that teachers must believe and enact. That is to say, we must help students master material, allow them to see that mastery (visible learning), and offer them the wonderful feeling of being successful. Allowing for "big wins," a focus on standards, and an insistence on high-quality work are prime examples.

## Big Wins!

One great strategy for helping make learning visible and building success for students is to help them make a few initial "big wins." My husband and teacher extraordinaire, John Wolfe, shared the concept of big wins with me. The basic idea is that teachers present students with a learning task that is reasonably challenging but with a bit of effort can be quickly mastered. John puts it this way:

> *Until kids see themselves having success, many don't believe it's even possible. Especially by the time they are in middle school. By then, some kids have experienced so much failure! So, to help them see themselves as capable learners we have to engineer success for them, we have to help them see "big wins" in their learning.*
>
> *For example, when I taught eighth grade language arts, I met a student, who I'll call Antoine. Antoine read at about the fourth grade level and thought of himself as a nonreader. I told him something that I always say when I meet kids who've struggled, "Don't worry, I'm a really good reading teacher and I'll make sure you leave my class reading well. You've got to do your part, Antoine, but if we work together and work hard, then you'll make a ton of progress." Antoine shook my hand but I could see he really didn't believe me. I knew I needed him to have a "big win" to see himself as successful. I also knew that if I worked with Antoine on fluency, reading rate in particular, he could make quick gains with a little bit of effort. Exactly what I wanted!*
>
> *I did a quick oral reading rate assessment, timed him for one minute and found that he read 76 correct words per minute on a passage at the fourth grade level. I recorded his score and talked with him about it. I told him that in general, when kids practice reading every day, they can increase their reading rate about two words per week. I asked Antoine to practice reading this passage and several others I gathered for him, every day for a week. Then at the end of that week I retested him on the same passage. He read 90 words per minute! He was thrilled! It really felt like a big win for him and he began to see himself as capable of growth. It was a great stepping off point for the goals we set the rest of that quarter.*

After John shared his theory with me, I wanted to try it myself. As an educator who has long focused on joyful learning, it occurred to me that when we feel proud of ourselves, joy is almost always a byproduct! I was working with a group of kindergarten teachers and we knew that getting a *big win* at this early educational age could help our students with learning for years to come.

We decided to help students see themselves as successful and capable through teaching them to tie their shoes. This may not sound like much, but shoe tying is hard; if you don't remember how hard, find a young friend and try teaching her or him how to do it. I'm not kidding – it's hard! But, doing hard things is important for building a sense of self-efficacy, pride in accomplishments, and a belief in potential. As the teachers and I worked with kiddos to learn to tie, we realized that an important outcome of our work was that students were learning that persistence pays off, that it is okay to do hard things, and most importantly, that they could achieve things that sometimes seem impossible (Platt, 2016).

As I watched students learn, I gave feedback focused on helping them learn to see the process as a metaphor for all that is possible in their lives as learners. I found myself encouraging them with other growth-mindset-focused ideas.

- *If you can learn to do this, you can do anything!*
- *You must feel so proud of yourself for continuing to try even when it was really hard!*
- *I know it's hard! I am here for you! Don't give up!*
- *Can you believe how hard you worked to make this happen?*

There is no way to overexpress how joyful the students were as they mastered shoe tying! They were so proud of themselves and truly beamed with success. For the rest of that year, as a motivation strategy, the teachers and I recalled the way our students felt after they had tried hard and been successful at tying their shoes.

> **Your Turn!**
> ★ Think of a time you've experienced students who were motivated by their success, or the opposite, think of students who were defeated by their perceived failures. How do those experiences relate to *visible learning* and *success breeding success*?
> ★ How could you help your students have big wins?

## A Quest for Quality

Before delving deeper into the concept of mastery, we will explore how to help students put forth effort in their daily work. I have been an educator for more than a quarter of a century, and in that time I have noted a growing problem. Students are turning in work that is lower and lower in quality. Not only is penmanship, punctuation, and spelling often poor, but often students seem to rush through their assignments, and the quality of their ideas, creativity, and other indicators of thoughtful work are poor also.

I am not complaining about "kids these days"! I love kids and they delight me daily with their insight. What I am saying is that as teachers, we have to inspire our students to do their best. I do not want the children I serve to bring error-ridden resumes to their prospective jobs. I want them to excel.

### What is quality?

To my mind, written work that is quality is:

- Correct
- Neat
- Thoughtful

Some teachers argue that asking students to write neatly and spell correctly can hinder creative content. Truly, I have not seen that to be the case. And, of course, I'm not talking about requiring perfection, either. But, I don't think it's too much to ask students to spell basic sight words correctly, use learned punctuation, and form their letters such that they can be read.

When teachers accept low-quality written work, they send powerful if inadvertent messages. Imagine a teacher, we'll call him Mr. Green, who accepts almost anything turned in, no matter how low quality. Here are some of the messages he is sending:

- Quality doesn't matter.
- I don't have to do my best.
- This assignment isn't important enough for me to work hard on it.
- Mr. Green doesn't think I can do any better.
- Mr. Green doesn't care about spelling, punctuation, or neatness.

These are not the messages most of us want to send. Additionally, as a teacher who expects and gets high-quality work from students, I know that students can be neat, correct, thoughtful, *and* creative all at the same time!

### Inspiring quality

Long-time educator and teacher leader Regie Routman (2018) wrote about the importance of holding students accountable for neat handwriting (p. 248), correct spelling (p. 240), and generally expecting students to work hard in her wonderful book *Literacy Essentials: Engagement, Excellence, and Equity for All Learners*. She wrote, "I believe one of the gravest educational injustices is how little we expect from our . . . students" (p. 259). That message resounded and energized me! I knew it was time to fight for high expectations for quality work from and for my students.

> You must unlearn what you have learned.
>
> – Yoda

I started with Yoda. Whether or not you are a big Star Wars fan (for the record, I am not), this quote is meaningful. For me, it speaks to the issue of quality and cuts to the core of my work as an educator. Teachers must coach for excellence, and often our students don't share that enthusiasm for carefully completed work. They have learned to cut corners, to do less, and to be content with poor penmanship, careless spelling, and other mistakes that take away from the overall quality of the work they do.

They must unlearn what they have learned.

A colleague of mine, Mrs. Clark, who is a much-loved teacher, starts the year with a strong message about what's to come in her class. Her message is similar to the one below.

*You are going to have a lot of fun this year! You will learn and grow and challenge yourself. I love you and will help you every step of the way. But, there is something you should know, I expect quality work. When you turn work in, it must be neat, correct, and thoughtful. If it's not, you will do it again. But, never think I'm punishing you! You will redo work for me and you will be proud of how you grow! I just know you will! You will leave my classroom feeling proud of your growth and knowing that I care very much about you.*

Powerful! In Chapter 2, you read about "branding," the practice of developing a unique identity for your classroom. Mrs. Clark's brand is clearly better for students than the brand suggested by Mr. Green's inadvertent messages.

### Ideas for supporting quality written work

Through the years, I have found several high-yield strategies for supporting high-quality work. I hope they prove helpful to you!

1. *Assign less but expect more.* Doing quality work takes time. I often hear teachers lament that their students don't have the time to make all of their work neat, correct, and thoughtful or that teachers don't have the time to have students redo work when it is low quality. Take a look at the work you assign students and ask yourself the following questions. If the answer to one or more of them is "no," then consider dropping the assignment or asking students to do it without handing it in. Work that is handed in should be high quality.
   - Is the work important to my overall goals for students?
   - Can the work be done orally? Does it need to be written?
   - If I ask students to complete the work, is there ample time for them to do it well and to revise it if needed?
   
   If the work will be handed in, consider allowing students to do some of it orally and some in written format. If, for example, a worksheet asks students to practice using textual evidence to support their answers to a text they read, only have students write out the answers to half of the questions.

2. *Give students tools.* No matter what grade you teach, students need simple tools to support them in doing quality work. I offer my students the following tools.
   - *Letter formation card*: A simple laminated half-sheet with correctly formed upper and lowercase letters for reference. Many students haven't ever been accountable for writing neatly and need the visual reminder. I keep them in a clip that hangs from the whiteboard so students can easily find them.
   - *Spacers*: I have found that many students do not put a space between their words. I offer them strips of cardboard that I've cut to be approximately an eighth of an inch thick and three inches long. Corn dog sticks also do the trick. They sit in a cup on my shelf and students use them when they need to.
   - *Portable word walls*: I give every student a copy of a folded 11 × 17 inch paper word wall with high-frequency words printed on it in alphabetical order. There is space for adding new words. When students lose them, I don't make a big deal of it, I just point in the direction of the extra copies. But, I do make a big deal when students spell simple words, like *because, their, what, where,* or *were,* incorrectly when they could have just used the portable word wall.

---

**My work is high QUALITY!**
- ❏ It is neat.
- ❏ It is complete.
- ❏ It is accurate.
  - ❏ Spelling is correct.
  - ❏ Punctuation is correct.
- ❏ I did my best!

3   *Collect work samples to use as anchor papers*. Students need visual examples of what quality work looks like. When you get high-quality work, save it, share it, maybe even post it on the wall. When students live up to the standards set by these anchor papers, celebrate with them! Have them tape the paper inside their binder as a reminder, take a picture and post it to your school's social media site, or text it to your student's parents. Later, if that same student offers lower-quality work, show them what you know they are capable of.

4   *Develop a* quality work *checklist for students*. I use the simple checklist in the gray box on page 62. Students tape it inside their folders and I ask them to read it over before they begin written work and again before they turn it in. I also have laminated copies available for students who have lost their own copies.

5   *Insist on students redoing work that is low quality*. Okay, this is the hardest suggestion. Go back and reread what Mrs. Clark tells her students at the beginning of each year and then take a deep breath. Asking students to redo work is hard. Sometimes they get mad. Sometimes they cry. But, it only takes redoing work once or twice for most students to realize that it's easier to just do it right the first time. When I find this aspect of my work hard to take, my husband, who is wiser than he is couth, says, "Embrace the suck!" What he means is that the hard parts are often the most important stops on the route to eventual success. He reminds me to celebrate the hard parts and think of them as a gift I give my students, a gift that will pay large dividends in the long run.

The key is to really work *with* students. Use each instance of low-quality work as an opportunity for one-on-one or small group lessons on what quality looks like and feels like. Working with students to revise and resubmit assignments can be exhausting and sometimes leads to weariness, but with nurturing and persistence, students learn our expectations and meet them and soon the possibilities for excellence seem endless!

## Focus on the Standards

The *big wins* strategy shared above focuses on using simple learning tasks to help students see themselves as capable of mastery and, as such, as capable of success. For more sustained experiences that lead to a mastery-based classroom, start with state learning standards.

It is time for us to admit to ourselves that even though teachers are superheroes, we can't do it all! That is why I advocate for a strong understanding of the standards your state has set forth for you and your students. For the most part, the Common Core State Standards are good. Even if your state doesn't use them, most state standards are very similar to the Common Core in English language arts and math. Further, the social studies, science, and so-called encore subjects (art, music, technology, physical education, etcetera) are similar across states as well.

It is incumbent on teachers to learn the standards they are charged with teaching and, for the most part, stick to them. Standards-based teaching supports mastery in two important ways.

1. **Standards allow for collaboration between teachers who serve the same students**. Even in elementary school, students are served by more than one teacher, never mind the great number of teachers that middle school, junior high, and high school students see. If we are all to be able to collaborate in the hope of helping students grow and learn, we need to be on the same page. Focusing on standards helps with that.
2. **Standards allow for articulation of very specific learning targets for student mastery**. Any given standard can be broken down into a series of learning targets. Each learning target can be shared with students along with the success criteria for meeting them, giving students a specific path to mastery and thus success!

Take for example the following standard, from the Common Core State Standards in English Language Arts, Informational Texts, Grade 6, Key Ideas and Details, Number 2:

*Determine a central idea of a text and how it is conveyed through particular details; provide a summary of the text distinct from personal opinions or judgments.*

The standard can be further broken down into learning targets (you can write them yourself or with a quick search, quality examples can be easily found on the web).
- *I can figure out the main idea of a text.*
- *I can find the key details that support the main idea.*
- *I can explain the main idea and how it is supported by key details.*
- *I can distinguish my opinion about a topic from the main idea of a text I read.*
- *I can coherently summarize informational text while leaving out my personal opinion.*

Once you have identified the learning targets embedded in a standard, you can share them with students along with the "success criteria" for meeting them. *Success criteria* is a fancy term for describing how the teacher and student will know when a given learning target has been mastered. The success criteria could be earning a certain percent on a test (for example, 90% or higher on a paper and pencil math test over studied concepts), a rubric, or a demonstrated ability to perform a given task (for example, a driving test).

The main idea is that standards can be used to motivate students, because they provide clear ways for students to see themselves mastering content. In recent years, there has been a push for teachers to post their learning targets on the wall for all to see. I have never been a fan of this method. Frankly, I have seen too many classrooms where the posted target does not match what is actually happening in the classroom. And, who can blame teachers? There are dozens of learning targets on deck on any given day in any given classroom! I do, however, strongly support sharing learning targets with students frequently and especially when they will be assessed. Think back to Chapter 2. There was a section on helping students understand the purpose of a lesson. There I shared the following three guiding questions for any lesson.

1  What am I learning?
2  Why am I learning it?
3  How will I know when I've learned it?

Clearly, the second question gets to the heart of purpose. The first and third help students understand the learning target and the success criteria. As I shared earlier, I have a colorful mini-poster featuring these guiding questions. I use it to remind myself and my students to think deeply about the learning expectations and keep them at the front of our thinking as we engage with new learning targets. To help you deepen your understanding of the process, read through the sample scripts below.

---

**Sample Learning Targets and Scripts for Sharing them with Students**

**Learning target:** I can figure out the main idea of a text.
*"Today we're going to work on figuring out the main idea of an informational text. This is important for many reasons and it's a skill you'll use for the rest of your life. You'll know that you have mastered this learning target when you can read a short nonfiction article and successfully find the main idea on three consecutive NewsELA (https://newsela.com/) articles. Soon you'll use your ability to determine the main idea to write a summary."*

> **Learning target:** I can give examples of how life changed for indigenous people after the conquistadors arrived.
>
> *"Students, you will soon be able to give examples of how life changed for indigenous people after the conquistadors arrived. We are going to read a short text and watch several video clips. Please look for examples of how life changed for indigenous people. Later, you'll use this information to help you form an opinion about whether the arrival of conquistadors was a good or a bad thing for the indigenous world. You'll know you've mastered the learning target if you can develop a list of at least five ways life changed."*
>
> **Learning target:** I can accurately describe the rock cycle.
>
> *"This week we will continue our study of the rock cycle. Your goal, at this point in our study, is to be able to accurately describe the cycle. When you can draw a detailed picture of the rock cycle, we'll know you've hit the target! Later, you'll use what you know to identify rocks in nature! It's a great hobby and really helps you learn to think deeply."*

> **Your Turn!**
> ★ Look at the sample learning targets and scripts in the box above. Can you identify how each of the guiding questions is addressed?
> ★ Find the state standards for your grade and/or content area and read them!
> ★ Work with a standard or two and try distilling them into learning targets and then scripting how you will present them to students, as in the example above.

The simple examples above show how sticking to standards can help teachers work with students on their ability to both master content and motivate them as they see themselves as learners capable of mastery!

### Simple Tips, Hints, and Ideas to Help Move Students to Mastery

Many of the ideas below were first introduced in Chapter 2. Here they are expanded on and looked at through a somewhat different lens. Helping students see themselves mastering content is inextricably linked to the topic of effort.

1 Teach students positive self-talk and a growth mindset!

*If you think you can or you think you can't, you're probably right.* I love this old saying. I share it with students and tell them even when they don't believe in themselves, I will believe enough for both of us! I teach students about the concept of growth mindset and help them with the words they will need to talk about their potential for doing high-quality work (see the table below, which can be used as an anchor chart.).

Words to help keep a growth mindset

| Instead of... | Try... |
| --- | --- |
| I'm not good at it. | I will try harder. |
| I don't get it. | What questions do I have? |
| I give up. | I will try again. |
| I can't do better. | I can always improve. |
| It's too hard. | It might take some time to finish. |
| I made a mistake. | Mistakes help me learn. |
| It's good enough. | Is it really my best work? |

2  Focus on the power of "yet!"

In *The Most Powerful 3-Letter Word a Parent or Teacher Can Use*, Daniel Coyle (2012) writes that "kids love to announce they're not good at something." One of the cures for this type of defeatism, says Coyle, is to teach children to add the word *yet* to the end of any such declarations. If, for example, one of my students says, "I can't do long division," I would encourage her to add *yet* to that statement, "I can't do long division yet." It's a small but powerful addition that almost forces the speaker into a growth mindset.

Help students practice using the subtle power of "yet"! When introducing learning targets, as shared above, ask students to try formatting with an eye for the future. Read through the examples below.

- *I can't figure out the main idea of a text yet, but I know Mrs. Platt will teach me and I'll be able to soon!*
- *Even though I can't give examples of how life changed for indigenous people after the conquistadors arrived yet, I will be able to after I read and think about the text on the topic.*
- *I can't yet describe the rock cycle, but I am excited to learn and soon I'll be able to talk about it like a professional scientist!*

## Goal Setting With Students

Growth mindset. Voice and choice. Student agency. Engagement, motivation, and ownership. These are just a few of the buzzwords that fly free in almost every professional development session I participate in. They have been used a few times in this very book! But often, there's not much behind the rhetoric. What does it mean to allow students voice and choice? What does agency look like? If you're like me, you want to know in a very practical way how we can get students engaged in choice-based academic growth that grounds idealism in daily practice. In Chapter 5, which focuses on differentiated instruction, you will encounter many strategies for voice and choice, but in the meantime, one answer is through goal setting.

Teaching students to set, monitor, and meet goals is a skill that they will be able to use for the rest of their lives. Goal setting helps build in purpose, mastery, and autonomy in a simple and very tangible way. When we teach students to set goals and then support them as they work to achieve those goals, we give them the gift of the pride and excitement that comes from knowing, beyond a shadow of a doubt, that they can work hard and achieve if they set their minds to it!

Goal setting allows for visible learning, and when students see their own success, it can open the door to more success. Remember the principle, "Success breeds success!" As a former principal of mine often said, "Goal setting is a prerequisite for happiness."

### A Step-by-step Plan for Teaching Goal Setting

There are as many ways to teach students to set, monitor, and meet their own academic goals as there are possible goals. Below is the method I use. You can use it whole cloth, modify it, or think of it as a springboard for devising your own plan.

> *STEP 1: Telling students why*
> Introduce students to the concept that they can "grow their brains." Researcher Carol Dweck compares the brain to a muscle and reminds students that they can grow their brains through exercise. To drive this home with students, I have them read the short article *You Can Grow Your Intelligence!* (Mindset Works, 2014). In a nutshell, this short read helps students understand the concept of growth mindset, how the brain is similar to a muscle, how connections are made, and how human beings can actually make themselves smarter.
>
> After we read the article, I lead a class discussion about the implications of research showing that human beings can actually raise their own IQs. Students really buy into it!

*STEP 2: Explain SMART goals*
Teach students about goals and why goal setting is important. I start by offering a student-friendly definition of the word *goal*.

*A goal is something that you work hard to be able to do.*

Further, I explain that a goal is like a promise we make to ourselves to accomplish something. I then teach students that if goals are to be successful, they must be SMART. SMART goals have long been the rage in teacher's circles, but the concept can also be harnessed to help students set strong goals. SMART is an acronym for Specific, Measurable, Attainable, Relevant, and Time-bound. Students must be taught to set goals that are SMART. I always give an example like the one below. Mrs. Shaw wanted to teach her students to set goals. She asked her students:

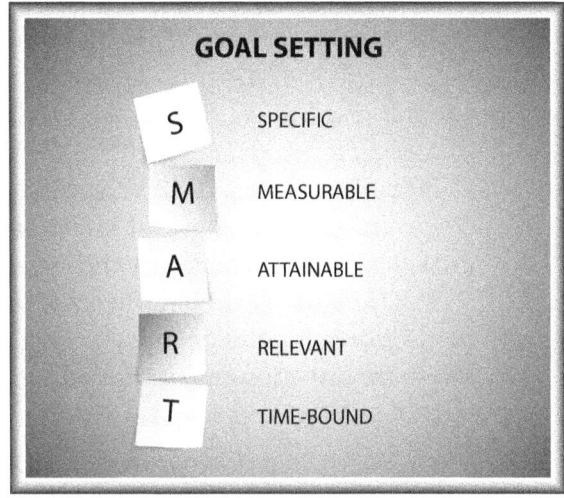

Figure 4.1 SMART goal defined.

*What if I wanted to set a goal to get more fit and I wrote it this way: "I will get fit!"*

*Is that a good goal? Probably not. Let's check to see if it's SMART.*
- *Is it specific? No! It doesn't tell what "fit" means.*
- *Is it measurable? No! There are no numbers in the goal at all.*
- *Is it attainable? Who knows? We're not even sure of what the goal means!*
- *Is it relevant? Probably, because being fit is good for almost everyone, right?*
- *Is it time-bound? No! There is no date included in the goal.*

*What if I wrote the goal this way:*

*"I will exercise at least three times per week by walking for 30 minutes each time. By the end of the month, I will have lost between one and two pounds." Is that a better goal? Yes! Much better, let's check to see if it's SMART.*

- *Is it specific? Yes! It tells what I am going to do, how often, and for how long.*

- Is it measurable? Yes! I can count the number of times I walk and check to see if I've lost weight.
- Is it attainable? Yes! It's not overly ambitious and it's doable for me.
- Is it relevant? Yes! I really need to shape up!
- Is it time-bound? Yes! I know how long I will work out and when to check for weight loss.

STEP 3: Practice with SMART goals

Once students have a solid grasp on what a SMART goal is, I share goal statements with them and we check them to see if they are SMART. I usually model one as a whole group and then have students work in pairs or fours to decide if the rest are SMART or not. We share our thoughts in the whole group as we hash each one out.

| GOAL | SMART? | RATIONALE |
|---|---|---|
| I will read 20 books by the end of the quarter (five novels a week). | No | Over ambitious. The goal is likely unattainable. SMART goals are ambitious but still very possible. |
| I will independently learn two new vocabulary words from the SAT list each week (20 words by the end of the second quarter). | Yes | It is specific (two SAT words), measurable (20 total), attainable (two per week), relevant (vocabulary is helpful for every aspect of learning), and time-bound (by the end of the second quarter). |
| I will learn more reading strategies. | No | Not SMART on any level. |

STEP 4: Write SMART goals!

Allow students to set their own goals! Ask them to think about the types of goals they would like to set. In my work as a teacher of English language arts, I always have students set a minimum of two. One is for number of books read and the other is for whatever aspect of their literacy lives they would like to work on. I share the following suggestions for my reading classes. There are no limits to the types of goals you can help your students set; this is just a beginner's list!

- *I will read five novels before April 30th.*
- *I will increase my oral reading rate from 70 WPM to 85 WPM by the end of the second quarter.*

- *I will read four books from three different genres by the end of the first quarter.*
- *I will finish the second Harry Potter book by winter break.*
- *I will collect and learn three new words a week during the month of April.*
- *I will practice analyzing poetry by independently analyzing four poems by the end of the year.*
- *I will write and publish four pieces of original material during the second trimester.*

*STEP 5: Help students be accountable*

Once students have determined and written down their goals, have them write down a plan to meet them. Remind them to check their own progress frequently. If kids (or adults!) are to meet their goals, they must be front and center. I often pair students with "accountability partners" they can check in with each day. These are just peers who are interested in helping other students meet goals. They simply check in with their partners from time to time and ask questions such as:

- *Hey, how's your goal work coming?*
- *Will you show me what you're doing to meet your goal?*
- *Is there any way I can help you in your work toward your goal?*

Another simple strategy is to have students "tap out" to show progress at the end of class. The door to my classroom has the numbers one through four taped onto the frame. Each number corresponds to a level on a rubric. I use the numbers for a variety of student self-assessment tasks. In the case of goal setting, the numbers stand for the following basic responses.

- 4 = I have already met my goal(s)!
- 3 = I am well on the way of meeting my goal(s)!
- 2 = I need to revisit my goal(s) and get busy!
- 1 = I am *way* behind on my goal(s)! *Help!*

As students walk out of the door at the end of class, they simply tap the number that best represents their progress toward meeting goals. I take note of any students who tap a two or one and confer with them individually to help them get on track.

Last, I hold students to working hard to accomplish their goals. When we confer, goals are at the heart of our conversations; when I talk to parents, I share goal progress. When the goal period is up, I assess to see that all students met goals. If they didn't, we problem solve together for next time.

In all accountability work, I remind students that a goal is a promise they make to themselves and my job is to help them keep it.

> **Your Turn!**
> - ★ Try setting your own SMART goal for reading, professional development, or your health.
> - ★ Think about the types of goals students could set in your classroom. Develop a possible list.
> - ★ Work with your students to set their own SMART goals.

### Simple Tips, Hints, and Ideas to Motivate Learners Through Goal Setting

Many of the ideas below were first introduced in Chapter 2. Here they are expanded on and looked at through a somewhat different lens. Helping students see themselves master content is inextricably linked to the topic of effort.

1. **Celebrate!**
   When students meet their goals, it's time to *celebrate* in simple but fun and powerful ways!
   - Pull out your cell phone and have students call home and share the good news!
   - Take students to see the principal or last year's teacher!
   - Give the student a hug, high-five, fist-bump, or elbow-touch (that last one is still weird to me . . .).
   - Give meaningful growth-mindset types of praise: *Wow! You worked hard to meet that goal! You must be so proud!* Or, *Good for you! What did you do that allowed you to meet your goal?*
   - Celebrate on social media! Post a picture of the student and a description of the accomplishment on the school's social media site.
   - Have a party! Invite all who worked hard to meet their goals.

2. **Keep families in the loop**
   Whenever possible, allow your students' parents and caregivers an opportunity to share in the goal-setting process. When I taught seventh grade reading, I always had students set goals and bring a copy of them home. Their assignment was to discuss their goals with their parents and ask for feedback. If parents had concerns or comments, they were asked to share them. Students revised goals with parent support when needed. I found this helpful in two ways. First, it helped parents feel more connected to the class and to helping their students meet their self-selected goals. Second, it allowed me a great way to start a conversation with parents and caregivers about student progress.

3  Use goal-setting forms

   Having an organized way to help students keep track of their goals and monitor their data is very helpful. I use a very simple goal-setting form. Students write their goal(s), their method of documenting progress, and their ideas for how to meet the goal(s). There is also space for students to record their success (or lack of success) at the end of the goal period. See the example below.

| **Name:** Raylene Patrone | **Class:** English 9, Period 2 |
|---|---|
| **SMART Goal 1:** I will read 5 novels by the end of the first quarter. | **SMART Goal 2:** I will learn 4 words from the SAT word list each week in the first quarter. |
| **Data for Progress Monitoring:** I will record the title of every book I read on the back of this sheet. I'll highlight the novels in yellow. | **Data for Progress Monitoring:** I will write the words and definitions in my notebook. I will ask an adult to quiz me on them every other week. |
| **Strategies to Meet the Goal:** <br>• I will pick books I want to read. <br>• I will read books with my BFF. <br>• I will read for at least 30 minutes each day after school. | **Strategies to Meet the Goal:** <br>• Choose words on Monday. <br>• Practice them every day for 5 minutes. <br>• Get my mom to work on them with me. |
| **Outcome:** I exceeded my goal! I finished seven novels! I am so proud of myself! | **Outcome:** I was supposed to learn 40 words but I only learned 30. I wrote all 40 in my notebook but couldn't remember the definition of 10 of them. |
| **Parent Signature:** Maria Patrone Gonzalez ||

4  Model by setting and sharing your own goals

   When you're asking students to set goals, it's helpful to be able to model setting and meeting your own. I use Goodreads to set a goal for the number of books I read each year and I share my progress with students often.

> **Recapping the BIG Idea**
>
> *When students realize they can master difficult content, they are more motivated and more joyful about learning.*
>
> **In this chapter we looked at:**
> 1. How the concept of mastery and increasing student effort leads to motivation.
> 2. Plans to implement strategies to help student increase the quality of the work they do.
> 3. Using standards-based lesson and learning targets to help students master content and see themselves as capable of effort-driven mastery.
> 4. Helping students set, monitor, and meet SMART goals.

**Mastery Makes a Difference**

Now that you have read this chapter, it should be clear to you that allowing students an organized way of demonstrating mastery of content is a powerful means to help build a classroom environment that is both filled with effort and is a joyful place to be.

# References

Carol Dweck/Mindset Works. (2014). Retrieved from https://www.mindsetworks.com/websitemedia/youcangrowyourintelligence.pdf

Coyle, D. (2012). *The most powerful 3-letter word a parent or teacher can use.* Retrieved from http://danielcoyle.com/2012/12/11/the-most-powerful-3-letter-word-a-parent-or-teacher-can-use/

Hattie, J. (2009). *Visible learning: A synthesis of over 800 meta-analyses relating to achievement.* London: Routledge.

Joelving, F. (2009). *How you learn more from success than failure.* Retrieved from www.scientificamerican.com/article/why-success-breeds-success/

Ladson-Billings, G. (2009). *The Dreamkeepers: Successful teachers of African American children.* 2nd Edition. San Francisco, CA: John Wiley & Sons.

Platt, R. (2016). *Once around the Bunny's ear: Shoe-tying as a metaphor for all that is possible.* Retrieved from www.weteachwelearn.org/2016/05/once-around-the-bunnys-ear-shoe-tying-as-a-metaphor-for-all-that-is-possible/

Routman, R. (2018). *Literacy essentials: Engagement, excellence, and equity for all learners.* Portland, ME: Stenhouse.

# 5

# Have it Your Way! Differentiated Instruction

> **The BIG Idea**
> *Differentiated instruction is simply about helping each student move forward as a learner. It does not have to be labor intensive or time consuming for teachers.*
>
> **In this chapter you will:**
> 1. Understand the basics of differentiated instruction and how it serves to support a happy and effortful classroom learning experience for students.
> 2. Learn to use voice and choice to increase students' sense of self-efficacy and their connections with the content they encounter.
> 3. Identify the ways to differentiate instruction by content, process, product, and environment.
> 4. Think about how differentiated instruction might impact the texts you offer students to read.

## Ode on a Boring In-service

Before I start writing about differentiated instruction for students and how it can help a classroom stay joyful and hardworking, I want to talk about professional development. I owe a lot to in-services. I met my husband, fellow educator John Wolfe, at one. I fell in love with the somewhat irritated-looking teacher at the back of the room who passed me a note sharing the poem he had just finished. It was, we later joked, an *ode on a boring in-service*. Read it on the next page.

**Low Song**

*By John Wolfe*

*(Composed and Revised during the October 5, 2010, Setting Priorities Staff Training Session, 10:00 to 11:30)*

*In dust-dark halls, I feel my days collapse.*
*Dawn's bright resolve drifts shuddering to gray.*
*Morning's bright yes devolves to dull perhaps.*
*Minutes, years, months, days, hours drift away.*
*If I could run – but who can hit top stride*
*When stones and brush and mud lurk underfoot*
*To pull you down, to swamp you in a tide*
*Of meetings, agendas barely understood?*
*Menus heap up, long days pass without food.*
*Thick shopping lists, we shuffle forth in rags.*
*Pale dreams with Bizness Speak are jagged glued.*
*Words bunch, boil over; slow the hour drags.*
*You wish for work like music smoothly flowing.*
*Your corporate jangle pop, a meek cow's lowing.*

**Image 5.1** John Wolfe bored at an odious inservice.

How many times have you found yourself in a boring in-service that seems to suck the soul right out of you, leaving you swamped in "tides of agendas barely understood"? I sure have. And more than once. Take a minute to reflect on why the professional development you are offered is less than meaningful and see if you come up with a list similar to mine, below.

> **When an in-service isn't meaningful it . . .**
> - Is one-size fits all.
> - Doesn't match what teachers think they need.
> - Seems to be focused more on getting a "pound of flesh" or "butt in the seat" time from teachers rather than on real job-related needs.
> - Is a "sit and get" session . . . where a presenter passes out papers and talks and teachers sit and listen.
> - Doesn't allow for peer interaction or cooperative learning.
> - Is negative and/or takes a scolding tone.
> - Is not connected to the teachers' or the school's goals and/or threatens to pull teachers in too many directions.

Now, think about your teaching. Does it match any of the descriptors above? Do you ever notice your students looking bored while you teach? Does the "bright resolve" of your students "drift shuddering to gray"? Does "morning's bright *yes* devolve to a dull *perhaps*"? If so, it's time to differentiate!

## What is Differentiated Instruction?

Differentiated instruction can be thought of as the way teachers meet the different learning needs of students in their classroom, or the way instruction is tailored to meet individual learning needs. Less succinctly, it can be defined as the way the teacher modifies the content, product, or process of teaching so that all students are challenged and can demonstrate academic growth, regardless of where they started.

Over the years, differentiated instruction has taken on a negative connotation for some teachers. Read below to see what one teacher had to say.

*Mr. Larcom is a ninth grade science teacher. He said, "I cringe when I hear the words 'differentiated instruction.' I feel like I've been told to differentiate for years but no one ever told me how. I don't have the time to personalize learning for every single student in every single class I have."*

Mr. Larcom isn't alone. Many teachers feel that the promise of differentiated instruction has not been fulfilled. But it can be. Truly, it is almost impossible to have a happy and effortful classroom climate without also using differentiated instruction.

*At its most basic level, differentiating instruction means "shaking up" what goes on in the classroom so that students have multiple options for taking in information, making sense of ideas, and expressing what they learn. In other words, a differentiated classroom provides different avenues to acquiring content, to processing or making sense of ideas, and to developing products so that each student can learn effectively.*

(Tomlinson, 2017)

Really, differentiated instruction is not a new concept; is it, plain and simple, good teaching. These days, a new term, *responsive teaching*, is getting a lot of buzz in education circles, but it has essentially the same meaning as differentiated instruction.

Differentiation is an idea with staying power. Many educational initiatives are directly related to differentiated instruction. Look at the chart below to see how.

| Initiative | How it is Related to Differentiated Instruction |
|---|---|
| **Response to Intervention (RTI)** | RTI aims to meet students at their need level with the goal of helping them move forward to catch up with their age-level peers. The idea is that all students can meet rigorous standards, but that they may need more time or different methods to do it. |
| **Professional Learning Communities (PLC)** | The PLC is built on a foundation of four questions (DuFour & Eaker, 2009):<br>• What do I expect my students to learn?<br>• How will I know when they've learned it?<br>• What will I do for those who do not learn it?<br>• What will I do for those who already know it or learn it quickly? |

| Initiative | How it is Related to Differentiated Instruction |
|---|---|
| | Note the last two questions call for educators to differentiate instruction for learners who either do not meet standards or have already mastered them. |
| Formative Assessment | The idea of formative assessment is to frequently check for each student's understanding of a given learning target, then use the results of the formative assessment to adjust instruction to meet individual, small group, and/or whole-class needs. |
| Special Education and Gifted and Talented Programs | Special education and gifted and talented programs are both premised on the idea that students can have learning needs that are quite different from those served entirely in the general classroom or without extra support. |

If you think back to the basic idea that differentiated instruction can be defined as *teaching to meet each student's needs*, can you see how the initiatives above are all deeply connected to differentiation?

## The Theory and Research

Differentiation can be a controversial topic. Some teachers balk at the very mention of it. Any quick internet search will come up with dozens of articles that offer support for both the idea that differentiation is essential for learning and the idea that differentiation doesn't work or is impossible to accomplish. I truly believe it does work but that often we make the concept too difficult. Most teachers differentiate daily. In my work observing teachers for more than 20 years, I have noticed that the most effective teachers differentiate as a matter of course.

The key thing to keep in mind is, as Larry Ferlazzo (2018) says, differentiation is not:

> *having to create a different lesson plan for each student in the room and long nights of planning and grading. That insanity is not what differentiation is all about. Differentiation is really a way of thinking, not a preplanned list*

*of strategies. Often times it is making decisions in the moment based on the mindset that all of our students bring different gifts and challenges. That as educators we need to recognize those differences and use our professional judgment to flexibly respond to them in our teaching.*

Let that last sentence sink in: "flexibly respond to [student needs] in our teaching." It is hard to argue that this type of mindset does not help teachers work to ensure that students meet standards.

## Voice and Choice

A great place to start a discussion on implementing differentiated instruction is with the concept of offering students voice and choice. Voice and choice is often referred to as *student agency* in the current education vernacular, and offering it to students is critical. The most joyful and hardworking classrooms are those where students are able to participate in making choices about how and what they learn, within the scope of the identified learning targets.

### How Voice and Choice Impact Motivation

In Chapter 2, you read about Dan Pink's deep dive into research about what motivates people to work hard. He distilled motivation research down to three factors: purpose, mastery, and autonomy. Autonomy was described as allowing for maximum self-determination. In the classroom, autonomy manifests in offering students voice and choice. Students, like all human beings, like to have options. One size does not fit all when it comes to learning.

When students have a sense of agency in school, they are more likely both to learn and to enjoy learning.

> *Time and again, research has shown that the more educators give students choice, control, challenge, and collaborative opportunities, the more motivation and engagement are likely to rise. The enhancement of agency has been linked to a variety of important educational outcomes, including: elevated achievement levels in marginalized student populations.*
>
> (Toshalis & Nakkula, 2012)

### Simple Tips, Hints, and Ideas to Allow for Voice and Choice

As you've seen above, offering students a modicum of choice can be powerful! Read through the ideas below with thoughts of how you can build more voice and choice into your teaching.

1  Surveying students
A good first step to offering students choice is to survey them on what they want, need, and like or don't like in school. Surveys can be as simple as asking students how they prefer to learn. That can be done through casual chat, by asking students to write about their learning needs, by using a premade survey online, or by making a survey for them to fill out. If you chose to make your own survey, try using www.surveymonkey.com or Google Forms; both platforms are free and very easy to use.
Examples of questions:

- Do you like to sit or stand?
- Do you like quiet or music in the background?
- What are your favorite ways to study?
- What subjects or topics do you enjoy the most?
- What is your favorite and least favorite thing about our class?
- What do you want to learn about?

Whatever survey you use, the key to motivating students to work hard is to use the survey results in visible ways, so they realize they do have voice and choice in their learning.

For example, one year I surveyed students on what they liked and didn't like about our language arts class. Over and over again, students wrote that they liked the course but did not like how I asked them to keep track of the vocabulary they were learning. I took that feedback to heart and shared it freely with my students. Together we brainstormed several possibilities for keeping track of vocabulary that met learning targets, my rigorous expectations, and students' needs for autonomy and choice. Win-win!

2  Build choice into assignments
Menus, bingo boards, learning contracts, and tiered assignments are all strategies for embedding choice into the assignments. Each will be explored in more depth below.

---

**Your Turn!**
- ★ Think about your own classroom. How do you allow for student voice and choice?
- ★ Do an internet search for student surveys or design one yourself. Give the survey to your students, analyze the results, and make some changes!

## Formative Assessment

Ongoing formative assessment is one of the essentials of meaningful differentiated instruction. Our differentiation decisions should grow out of a solid understanding of what students already know and what they need to learn.

Formative assessments are simple, often very quick learning probes that help you answer the question, *what do my students know and what do they still need to learn?* Or even more simply put, *are they getting it?*

Formative assessment is *not* new! You're doing it now! If you do any of the following and use the results to guide your teaching, you are already formatively assessing!

- Observe students as they work.
- Listen to the questions students ask and the answers they give.
- Give quizzes.
- Grade or check worksheets.

Most teachers apply these types of assessments naturally and frequently as they observe students, check their work, and question them. But research has shown that formative assessment is even more effective if planned in advance with an eye toward identifying specific learning needs (Popham, 2009).

### Simple Tips, Hints, and Ideas for Formative Assessment

Below are five examples of quick and simple formative assessments that can be easily built into your teaching and can help you discover what your students know in relation to a learning target.

1  Exit tickets

   This simple assessment strategy can be helpful in any subject, with any age student, and is quick and easy to implement. To use it, think of a question, a problem, or a point to ponder – something about which you'd like students to share their knowledge. Write a prompt on the whiteboard, or have premade copies for each student, and ask students to respond in writing to the prompt before they leave class. Their written answers are their "exit tickets" out the door!

   For younger students or English language learners, diagrams and multiple choices are often good adaptations. The possibilities are limitless. Teaching math? Ask students to do one problem or explain how to solve a problem. Teaching English language arts? Ask students to define a term, write a six-word theme, or describe a character trait. Teaching science or social studies? Ask students to summarize a concept, diagram a process, sketch a map, or compare and contrast two points.

Of course, exit tickets should be designed so they target key information and, as such, help teachers gain insight into each student's and the entire class's knowledge and level of understanding in relation to a given learning target. Make sure exit tickets are quick and easy to develop, administer, and grade. Also, don't let the name fool you – "exit tickets" can be used at any time during class. Call them "admit tickets" at the start of class and "check-in tickets" mid-lesson.

2  3, 2, 1 Quick write
This formative assessment can be used orally or in writing and, like an exit ticket, can happen in any subject with any topic. The teacher asks students to share by telling *three* things, then *two* things, then *one* thing. For example, a teacher whose class is working on learning the rock cycle in science might ask for three facts about the rock cycle, two ways it connects to the last unit, and one question that still needs to be answered or one point that needs to be clarified. Or a math teacher might ask for three examples of fractions in real life, two different ways to show a fraction, and one thing that is still confusing.

3  Self-assessment
Teaching students to self-assess and share the results with you is a powerful way not only to learn about how well each child understands a topic, but also to give students a sense of voice and self-efficacy. Ask students to reflect on how well they understood a lesson or a topic. Then have students share that reflection in a variety of ways. I like to tape numbers to my door jamb and, as students leave, ask them to "tap-out" by touching the number that corresponds with their self-assessed levels. Four means, "I totally get it! I could teach it to others!" Three means, "I understand it and feel confident." Two means, "I need a little help." One means, "I really don't get it! Please show me again!"

Two similar and fun methods use the same set of four "understanding" descriptors, but instead of tapping out, students use colored sticker dots (like those used for pricing items at a garage sale) or sticky notes. With sticky notes, students write their name or initials on a single sheet and then post it on a wall or a table marked with the levels of understanding. For example, a teacher might have four pieces of chart paper posted on each wall. The first chart would be labeled, "I got this!" The second, "I'm getting it! No worries!" The third, "Nope. Not getting it." The fourth, "What? I was supposed to learn what?"

Students then affix their notes to the poster that best describes their level of knowledge on the topic with the number that represents their understanding. Using colored stickers, students can choose a color and

Image 5.2 Tapping out to self-assess.

stick it to a predefined spot or on a worksheet they have completed. A green means, "I do not need help!" A yellow means, "I'm well on my way." A red means, "I need more practice or *help*!" This can be modified for students to use during quiet independent work. All students need is a card that is green on one side and red on the other. If all is going well, the green side should be face up on their desks. If there is trouble, the red card should be face up as a signal for the teacher to help as soon as she or he can.

4  Simple checklists
   The teacher uses a checklist to mark student progress toward learning targets as she or he confers one on one with students or watches them

work. The checklist can simply list skills needed to reach a target and can be carried around on a clipboard or, as I use them, on an iPad. As teachers observe and confer with students, skills they have mastered are checked off. The checklist can help with planning for future lessons. The example shows a checklist I used when the learning target was for students to write a theme statement for a fiction text.

| | Goals | Problem/ Solution | Beginning/ Middle/ End | Author's Purpose | Theme Word | Theme Statement |
|---|---|---|---|---|---|---|
| Copland | 50 | ✓ | ✓ | ☐ | ☐ | ☐ |
| Sam | 65 | ✓ | ☐ | ☐ | ☐ | ☐ |
| Liv | 60 | ✓ | ✓ | ☐ | ☐ | ☐ |
| Shwarnim | 63 | ✓ | ✓ | ✓ | ☐ | ☐ |
| Abi | 48 | ✓ | ✓ | ✓ | ✓ | ☐ |
| Kennedy | 50 | ☐ | ✓ | ✓ | ☐ | ☐ |
| Catherine | 53 | ✓ | ✓ | ☐ | ☐ | ☐ |
| Jocelyn | 55 | ✓ | ✓ | ☐ | ☐ | ☐ |
| Gabe | 28 | ☐ | ✓ | ✓ | ☐ | ☐ |
| Olivia S | 30 | ✓ | ✓ | ☐ | ☐ | ☐ |
| Owen | 25 | ✓ | ✓ | ✓ | ☐ | ☐ |
| Larissa | 30 | ✓ | ✓ | ☐ | ☐ | ☐ |

Image 5.3 Sample checklist.

5 Google forms

There are a great many wonderful (and free) platforms for formative assessments on the internet or as apps for phones and tablets. Kahoot!, Quizizz, Socrative, and Poll Everywhere are good sites to check out. However, these platforms seem to come and go quickly. Google Forms is likely to be around for a long time. To use Google Forms, you need a free Gmail account. Once you're logged in to your email account, look for the link to Google Apps and select "Forms." If you don't see that choice, click on "More" to find it. Create a new form, and you will be guided through adding questions that can be answered as short answer, a paragraph, multiple choice, checklist, etc. Google Forms are incredibly easy to create, and the data collected from a form can be exported to a Google Sheet (like Excel) where it is self-graded and easily analyzed.

## Types of Differentiation

Differentiation guru Carol Ann Tomlinson explains that we can think of differentiation in four categories: content, process, product, and learning environment (Tomlinson & Moon, 2014). Simple definitions for each category are described below.

Differentiation by:

- *Content:* What students are learning and the materials they use to learn it.
- *Process:* How students learn content, the methods and activities that are used to support learning.
- *Product:* How students demonstrate their learning, how they are assessed, what projects they complete.
- *Learning Environment:* Where and how students learn in the physical environment.

The chart below offers a deeper look at each category of differentiation along with examples of it in action. As you peruse the chart, think about how you currently differentiate or how you feel you could or should differentiate in the future.

| Type of Differentiation | Questions it Answers | Examples |
| --- | --- | --- |
| Content | <ul><li>What are the standards?</li><li>What are the learning targets?</li><li>What will students use as a vehicle for meeting targets?</li><li>What will they do?</li><li>What materials will teachers share?</li></ul> | <ul><li>Modifying learning targets to match student level.</li><li>Allowing students to meet standards while studying different content (i.e., if the learning target is to read and understand primary sources, allowing the students to choose which primary source they read).</li><li>Using books on a given subject at multiple reading levels.</li><li>Assigning different problem sets in math depending on what students need to practice.</li></ul> |

| Type of Differentiation | Questions it Answers | Examples |
|---|---|---|
| | | • Allowing students to choose their own research topics.<br>• Giving students worksheets/activities at different levels of readiness or complexity. |
| **Process** | • *How will they do it?*<br>• *What activities will they participate in?* | • Using manipulatives or other scaffolding material to help a student learn.<br>• Allowing for extra time.<br>• Using different and flexible grouping strategies.<br>• Using peer tutoring.<br>• Delivering content differently (lecture, hands-on methods, video, etc.).<br>• Offering varied types of learning activities. |
| **Product** | • *What will students turn in?*<br>• *How will students show they've met learning targets?* | • Allowing students to demonstrate their knowledge in different ways.<br>• Using different rubrics adjusted by student need.<br>• Allowing students to work together on final products.<br>• Using contracts or to-do lists based on needs.<br>• Allowing for choices in final projects or assessments. |
| **Environment** | • *Where will they work?*<br>• *How will the room be used to meet students' needs?* | • Making sure there are different spaces in the room that allow for solo, group, or pair work.<br>• Allowing students to stand up or move while working.<br>• Using flexible seating choices. |

## Steps to Differentiation

One of the major complaints I've heard from teachers is that they have been told frequently to differentiate but have not been given training on what that means. As I've noted previously, differentiation should not be a scary topic; really and truly, it is just what effective teachers have always done. It is working with students to help them learn in ways that work best for them. In that spirit, I offer the following steps to help you work to differentiate instruction in your classroom.

1. *Define your learning targets.* Think back to Chapter 4 and the topic of mastery. If differentiation is to be successful, teachers must be knowledgeable about state and district standards and benchmarks. Before designing a unit or a lesson to use as a base for differentiation, you must have the end goals in mind. If you can't answer the following questions, you might want to consult your state standards and redefine your learning targets.
   - What am I trying to teach?
   - What should students know and be able to do as a result of the lesson or unit?
   - Why am I teaching it?
   - Where does this fall into the scope and sequence for the whole year?
   - How will I know when my students have mastered the learning targets?
2. *Assess your students in relation to the learning target.* Before we teach to students' needs, we have to know what those needs are. To find out what your students already know and still need to know, a pre-assessment is helpful.

   The assessments can take many forms. From a pretest to a quick write to an informal question-and-answer period, there are many effective ways to find out what a student knows. Below, in the section on formative assessment, are several examples.
3. *Review the assessment results and think about your students' needs.* Before you plan the basic lesson and add modifications for different students or groups of students, reflect on the data you gathered using the four essential questions of a professional learning community (Dufour, Dufour, Eaker, & Many, 2006).
   - *What do I expect my students to learn?*
   - *How will I know when they've learned it?*
   - *What will I do for those who do not learn it?*
   - *What will I do for those who already know it or learn it quickly?*

4   *Develop plans to meet the needs* using differentiated content and/or process. See the example below.

**Step 1:** Miss Gudmunsen (not her real name) teaches fifth grade social studies. Her state standards call for students to *compare the different amounts of freedom held by different groups in Colonial America including but not limited to American Indians, landowners, women, indentured servants, enslaved people, and children in each group*. Miss Gudmunsen determines that the learning targets include all of the following:

- *Understand the concept of freedom.*
- *Identify major groups living in America during Colonial times.*
- *Describe the extent to which each group was or wasn't free.*

She realizes that students must master the learning targets so that they will be able to understand information in future units on the Revolutionary and Civil wars. Miss Gudmunsen knows that understanding relative levels of freedom will be very important to mastering future social studies learning targets.

| Knowledge | Questions |
| --- | --- |
| Slaves were not free. | What are indentured servants? |
| Women didn't have equal rights. | Were landowners only white? Did women own land? |
| Native American were free. | Were Native Americans ever enslaved? |

**Step 2:** Miss Gudmunsen begins the unit by asking students to complete a formative assessment that includes a quick write on the question, *What does it mean to be free?* and a Knowledge/Question (KQ) chart (as seen in the example above).

**Step 3:** She looks at what each student wrote and determines that some students have very little background knowledge on Colonial American groups while others know quite a bit. She also finds that the questions students asked on the KQ chart indicate differing areas of curiosity. Last, she realizes that the students need several common points of reference including shared vocabulary and a basic background of the historical era. From past experience with her students, Miss Gudmunsen knows that some prefer to learn through reading while others prefer using graphic and visual information.

**Step 4:** Miss Gudmunsen plans the following differentiated activities and methods to meet the second learning target ("Identify major groups living in America during Colonial times").

1. Small group pre-teaching to help students who showed limited knowledge review or to learn the basics of Colonial times in America.
2. Whole group vocabulary lesson (Terms: colonial, era, freedom, servitude, slave, landholder, indentured servant, social classes).
3. Small group background building on major groups living in America during Colonial times: Group 1 reads a short text, Group 2 analyzes period art, Group 3 watches a short video.
4. Small group jigsaws where members from each group above work together in new mixed groups (members to include representatives from Group 1, Group 2, and Group 3 above) to share the knowledge they gained.
5. Demonstration of knowledge where students can individually or collaboratively show they can identify major groups in a written or visual format or through a brief oral presentation.
6. Deeper learning experience by providing opportunity for students to choose a group they are interested in, research it, and develop a short presentation on the group using a visual, written, or oral format.

## Simple Tips, Hints, and Ideas for Differentiation

After reading about the *whats* and *whys* of differentiation, you're probably ready for some practical *hows*! Read on to see three examples of stress-free, low-prep ways to differentiate.

---

**Your Turn!**

★ As you read the example from Miss Gudmunsen's classroom, think about how it resonates with your own experiences differentiating instruction. Are there any aspects you want to incorporate into your teaching?

★ Think about your classroom and identify ways you differentiate by content, process, product, and environment.

★ Choose a learning target and try using the differentiation steps to make a plan to help students meet the target.

1  Tic-Tac-Toe boards (differentiation by process and product)
   This is a great way to help students make choices while still meeting learning targets. After determining a learning target, the teacher uses a three by three grid. Each box on the grid is filled in with a different choice for learning the content, meeting the learning target, and/or showing that the target has been met. The choices offered must include a variety of methods and experiences.

   Students are required to pick and complete at least three activities and may choose to do more if they like, or they may be required by the teacher to do more if more practice is needed. Tic-Tac-Toe boards can be used as a pre-learning experience, as part of the main learning, or as a way to assess learning at the end of a lesson or unit. Look at the examples below.

*Example 1: Practice of a Math Concept,* Graphing Ordered Pairs, *After the Initial Lesson Set*
Notice that to get three in a row, the student must complete practice problems. It was designed that way because while the teacher wanted to offer the students choice, she also wanted them to do several practice problems as a part of their learning.

| Watch two Khan Academy videos on graphing ordered pairs (bookmarked on our class website). | Play "Give Me an Ordered Pair"! Use the grid on the floor in the back of the classroom. Pick an ordered pair slip from the bucket and walk to it. Have a partner check you. If you're correct, you get a point! | Do the problems on the worksheet. Check your answers with the teacher when you are done. Correct your mistakes. |
|---|---|---|
| Find a partner and use the USA maps to choose two places you each wish to visit. Determine the coordinates for the borders and write them down. Switch papers with your partner, then race to see who finds the other's travel destinations first. | Do the odd problems on page 123 in your math book. Check your answers with a partner. Correct your mistakes. | Play "Catch the Fly" on an iPad. Your avatar is a frog. A fly will land on a graph and you will key in the ordered pair. If you're correct, you get to eat a yummy fly and level up! |
| Write a *short* children's book that tells and shows kids how to use ordered pairs to find a spot on a grid. *Or* draw a pirate map of the room; choose a spot for buried treasure. Make a three-step set of coordinate directions to help someone else find the treasure! | Make an ordered pair picture for a classmate. Use graph paper to draw a simple geometric shape with at least five sides. Put a point at each angle. Write the ordered pairs on another sheet of paper. | Do the even problems on page 123 in your math book. Check your answers using the key. Correct your mistakes. |

*Example 2: Building Background for a Social Studies Unit on Native American Tribes*

| Do an internet search for a map of Native American tribes in North America in the 1500s, the 1800s, and today. Also, compare population numbers in these times. Make a Venn diagram and show how distribution and population of Native American people compares and contrasts from 1500 to 1800. | View the image galleries that show Native Americans in the past and in modern times. Do a quick write that speaks to the prompts below for each set of photos.<br>• I noticed …<br>• I am fascinated by …<br>• I wonder …<br>• I am surprised that … | Peruse the list of words that are commonly used today that have Native American origins. Chose eight to ten of them and use them in sentences. Find a friend to read the sentences to and ask them to use context to figure out what the words mean. |
|---|---|---|
| Choose a video from the links provided and watch it. Do a 3, 2, 1 Quick write:<br>3 Things you learned<br>2 Things you want to learn more about<br>1 Question you have about Native Americans of the past or today. | Read your textbook and answer at least three of the questions at the end of the chapter in writing. Do not forget to restate the question in your answer and support it with evidence. | Surf the internet links (found on our class website) exploring the modern day lives of Native Americans. Draw a picture or make a mind-map that helps you explore your thoughts on what you've learned. |
| Examine the books of Native American art. Read the captions. Choose two art pieces or art styles that you appreciate and try doing a quick sketch in a similar style. Write a caption for each that gives information you learned in the book and tells why the art or style is meaningful to you. | Do the "By the Numbers" Worksheet. Use the table that shares demographic information about Native Americans in the past and today. Answer the questions on the worksheet. | Using a blank sheet of paper, sketch pictures of everything you think you know about the history of Native Americans (feel free to add words). Cut the pictures out and sort them into categories (clothes, food, houses, daily life, war, etc.). Then choose one thing from each category and use books or the internet to verify or refute what you think you know. |

2 HyperDocs (differentiation by process and product)
HyperDocs are online blended learning opportunities made by teachers. The creators of HyperDocs invented "the term to describe the digital lesson design and delivery of instruction that was happening in our classrooms" (Highfill, Hilton, & Landis, 2016, p. 7). Think of them as online documents that allow learners to access information and show their understanding in a variety of ways using links to websites, videos, and texts.

A HyperDoc can be used in a way that is very similar to Tic-Tac-Toe boards shown above. If you want access to a HyperDoc I created, I will happily share! Also, visit Teachers Give Teachers, a website developed and maintained by the creators of the HyperDoc concept. After creating a free account, you can use any of the HyperDocs created by fellow educators. www.hyperdocs.co/teachers_give_teachers

3 Tiered assignments (differentiation by content, process, and product)
This is a strategy designed to meet the needs of learners at multiple levels. Each "tier" refers to a level of the assignment that meets the needs of a group of students at a certain readiness, skill, or level of proficiency. Using the words of common standardized texts, you can think of this as below-level or basic, on-level or grade-level, and above-level or advanced learners. You would never want to use them with your students in this context, however, as it can lead to a negative mindset that blocks growth (see "Caution" box).

Below you will find an example of tiered assignments for a math practice where the learning target is to add and subtract fractions with unlike denominators. The tiers are practice activities that a teacher can offer students after s/he has provided whole group or small group direct instruction. Notice that at each tier, the assignment becomes more complex.

- *Tier I: Basic Learners*: Review the concept by watching the Khan Academy video on adding fractions with unlike denominators. Complete odd-numbered problems on the practice worksheet at the back table with the teacher. Work with the Tier II group to model a problem with Legos.
- *Tier II: Grade-Level Learners*: Students will complete the worksheet with practice activities independently or with a partner who is also working in Tier II. When done, the teacher will check the answers.

Once errors (if any) are corrected, students will choose one problem from the worksheet to model with Legos on their own and one to model with a partner from the Tier I group.
- *Tier III: Advanced Learners*: Students will complete the worksheet with practice activities. Once complete, students will compare their answers with another student who in working in Tier III. If there are discrepancies, students will work together to determine who is correct. Next, student pairs will work together to brainstorm real-world examples of the need to add and subtract fractions, write the examples as story problems, switch problems with another pair, and solve one another's problems, modeling at least one with Legos.

I recently saw a teacher using tiered assignments connected with student voice and choice in their English language arts classroom. Read about the lesson I saw in Mr. Movar's (not his real name) room.

*As Mr. Movar finishes the whole-class lesson on finding theme, he asks the students to do a quick formative assessment. He says, "Now that we've all had some basic instruction on finding theme in a short story, it's time to practice. First, show me how good you feel about your ability to find theme. Give me a thumbs up if you're confident, a thumb's sideways if you feel like you're on your way to being confident but need a little more guided practice. Last, give me a thumbs down if you really feel that you don't 'get' the theme yet." As the students score themselves, Mr. Movar takes note.*

*Then he gives directions for the practice segment of the lesson. "Okay! It looks like we're all over the place in terms of understanding. Let's use three groups. If you gave a thumbs up and truly feel confident, please go to the back of the room and choose one of the picture books from the bin you find there. Read it, think about the theme, and then write a theme statement that uses evidence from the text to support the author's message you inferred. Group two, you are feeling partially confident. With a little more instruction, you might find you're ready to give a thumbs up. You will go to the computer lab. Look on my webpage. I made two videos that I believe will help you. Watch them and then click the link for the short practice. You'll read really short stories and choose a theme for each multiple choice style. Keep track of how many you get wrong. If you miss more than one or two answers, you'll want to come talk to me so I can offer further instruction. If you put your thumb down, you probably want to join me at the front table for some reteaching! I will help you and I promise you'll get it, it just might take a little more time."*

While I watched, the students in Mr. Movar's class sorted themselves as they felt appropriate and got to work. It was an amazing display of self-assessment, differentiated instruction, and a happy, hardworking classroom!

> Also, of course, never refer to students by a level. The tiers in this example are labeled for teacher learning only. In the classroom I would call them Blue Group, Green Group, and Yellow Group, or Hearts, Smiles, and Peace Signs, or any other nonhierarchical name. Students should not think of themselves as a level. It can be damaging in many ways.

### 4  Flexible seating (differentiation by process and product)

Having flexible work areas can be a powerful aspect of differentiated instruction. Middle school teacher Brooke Markle (2018) puts it this way,

*Flexible seating is about more than simply having a variety of different, fun seats in the classroom. It's about utilizing student voice, creating buy-in, heightening collaborative learning, and prioritizing students' needs concerning the environment in which they learn.*

Seating choices can make or break a student's ability to work happily and productively. Some students need quiet places to work; others need to move. Some prefer to sit, while others prefer to stand. This is easy for us to accept when it comes to adults.

Think about where you work best. How does it compare to the common classroom desk? If you're like most people, a classroom desk, even if it were big enough to accommodate an adult-sized person, isn't ideal. Personally, I do my best work in my bedroom (I know, I know, work-life-balance problems). I often work long after my kids have gone to sleep.

In Chapter 1, you read about Mrs. Miner's classroom as a model of an environment that fostered happy and hardworking learners. There are many options for flexible seating. The best have the following elements.

- "Home bases" or assigned spots for students to sit when needed.
- Varied seating (or standing) choices. Teachers at my school offer low tables, standing desks or counters, wobble chairs, yoga ball seats, open learning spaces for group work, quiet learning areas (often with study carrels), lap desks, pillows, couches, and/or comfortable chairs.
- Personal touches including photographs, lamps, and other homey items.

**Your Turn!**
- ★ Choose one of the methods for differentiation shared above and search for more examples on the internet.
- ★ Develop and teach using a differentiated lesson you found online or made on your own.
- ★ Survey your students on how they liked the learning experience.

Images 5.4–5.8 Flexible seating options.

Images 5.4–5.8 Continued

Images 5.4–5.8 Continued

## The Role of Reading in Differentiated Instruction

For most of my career as an educator, I have focused on literacy as a driver for academic success. As such, it would be impossible for me to write about differentiated instruction without including a section on meeting students' individual needs in reading.

The key to differentiated instruction of content and process is taking individual students' needs and/or interests into account and planning to meet them. When it comes to reading, students must have access to texts that they can read. Sometimes that means scaffolding such that students have access to difficult texts, and other times that means using texts that fall into that sweet spot where they are neither too challenging nor too easy but they are just right.

### Two Categories of Texts

Almost all classes require some reading. There is evidence to suggest that students should be exposed both to challenging texts, even those that might frustrate students a bit (Shanahan, 2017), and to texts that fit at that just-right level where the reading is neither too hard nor too easy (Allington, 2013).

A frustration of mine is that in our profession, hard lines are often drawn and false dichotomies are born. There is a kind of do-this-but-*never*-do-that feel on blogs, Twitter, and conference sessions that often leaves me confused and feeling bad. Some of us are old enough to remember the pinnacle of this type of either-or thinking when classroom teachers became pawns of "the reading wars". At that time, the fight was whether to use a systematic phonics-based approach to teaching reading or to use a whole-language approach. Of course, the reality was that then, as now, classroom teachers used an approach that was not completely one or the other, but rather a so-called balanced approach that used tenets and strategies from both ends of the spectrum.

Today, that war seems to be stoking again, but at the center is the argument about whether to use grade-level texts (with support), texts that are at a given student's instructional level (can be read with scaffolding) or independent level texts (can be read with almost no support).

Once again, however, it is likely that the best practice lies somewhere in the middle, or as the National Education Association (2017) puts it,

> *A complete reading program is analogous in several ways to a balanced diet. [It] is achieved by providing diverse components in ratios that are not necessarily equal. In addition, the ratios might vary with individual needs and with development. For example, infants do not eat five servings of fruits and vegetables as recommended for children and adults. In a similar fashion, beginning*

*readers might require different amounts of certain types of reading activities than more proficient readers.*

The bottom line is that excellent teachers make flexible choices that help meet the different needs of each unique learner. That means that sometimes our students should be reading grade-level texts even if they are difficult and sometimes they should be reading texts that best fit their own reading levels.

Glasswell and Ford (2010) speak to the idea of a balanced approach where teachers use "varying instructional support and varying text levels. In an engaging and challenging classroom, the teacher carefully decides the degree of instructional support needed for readers to engage in the text selected."

**Simple Tips, Hints, and Ideas for Differentiated Instruction with Grade-level Texts**
Before sharing strategies for teaching with grade-level texts, I have two caveats to consider.

One, the idea of "grade-level" is mushy as best. Texts can be analyzed in a variety of ways, and determining an exact level is impossible. When thinking about the level of a given text or reader, add the word "ballpark." The book's level is in the *ballpark* of an average ninth grader. Or the student reads easily in the *ballpark* of an average fifth grader.

Two, the texts we use in our classes aren't necessarily even in the grade-level ballpark. In fact, reading expert (and one of my personal heroes!) Richard Allington (2002) shared research that showed that textbooks are often written two to three levels above what would be considered appropriate for the age of the average students reading it. He writes,

> *Even students who read on grade level may have trouble learning from their textbooks. Historically, a 95–97 percent accuracy level has been considered appropriate for instructional texts (Harris & Sipay, 1990). But texts of this level of difficulty are simply too hard for assigned content-area reading. Consider that a student reading a book at his or her "instructional reading level" will misread or skip as many as 5 words of every 100. In a grade-level high school science or social studies text, then, students will misread 10–25 words on every page! They won't misread* if, runs, locate, *or even* misrepresent, *but rather unfamiliar technical vocabulary specific to the content area, such as* metamorphosis, estuary, disenfranchised, *and* unicameral.

(p. 17)

Now for the tips!

1  **Don't just assign – teach**
   Given the information above and the wide range of readers found in most classrooms, simply telling students what pages to read and what questions to answer must be a practice driven into extinction. Instead, try teaching the text selection in a whole group or small group setting. Stop students frequently to ask questions and to monitor their comprehension.

2  **Intentional partner reading**
   Pair readers who struggle with readers who are proficient for assigned classroom readings. Paired reading harnesses social power, reading professor Timothy Shanahan (2018) notes,
   - *When it comes to learning the content of the texts, one usually does better reading with social support than on one's own, and that advantage is heightened when the texts are more difficult, the content less familiar, or an individual's internal motivation is attenuated.*
   - *Social interactions about texts tend to sharpen our game: having someone to talk to about a book improves comprehension (whether those others are book club buddies, or a teacher hired for that purpose). Social partners can push a reader to reflect more deeply or more thoroughly about ideas, or to notice things that may have escaped them if left to their own devices.*
   
   To insure that paired reading is focused and effortful, teach students to use a partner reading protocol like the one I use (shown below).

3  **Pre-teach vocabulary**
   As noted above, when students are asked to read challenging texts, there can be a tendency to blow past unknown words. To combat that tendency, teachers can teach words that are essential to comprehending the text. Pre-read what you want students to later read and highlight the words that you think must be understood. Then, take a class period to teach the words and let your students practice them. Make mini custom glossaries with student-friendly definitions that students can quickly and easily access. Allow them to use mini-glossaries you or they make while reading the text.

4  **Teach SQ3R**
   Helping students stay tuned into the text they are reading is critical. Strategies used before, during, and after reading can keep students focused. SQ3R is a good strategy to start with. Teach SQR and then require and remind students to use it. The anchor chart below may be helpful.

## Partner Reading Rules

### 1. Sit closely

You need to be able to hear each other

### 2. Take turns

Read by paragraph or by page if the pages are short.

### 3. Follow along!

If Partner A is reading, Partner B is following with a finger, listening, & thinking!
If Partner B is reading, Partner A is following with a finger, listening, & thinking!

### 4. Ask your partner to tell you what you read!

When Partner A is finished reading a paragraph, he or she turns to Partner B and says, "Did you understand what I read?" Partner B summarizes what was read. Then, Partner B reads and asks Partner A, "Did you understand waht I read?" Partner A summarizes what was read.

Image 5.9 Partner Reading Rules anchor chart.

| SQ3R | |
|---|---|
| Survey | Survey the text. Carefully examine all of the text features you find including headings, chapter titles, captions, summaries, and questions. Study the pictures, charts, and other graphics. Ask yourself what you already know about the topic. |
| Question | Ask yourself, "What am I going to learn?" Turn section headings into questions too! For example, if a chapter is called "Artificial Intelligence: Promises and Perils," ask yourself, "What are the promises of AI? What are the perils?" |
| Read | Read the text paragraph by paragraph. At the end of each paragraph ask, "Did I understand what I read?" Then summarize the content. As you read, look for answers to the questions you developed above. |

| SQ3R | |
|---|---|
| Recite | When you have finished a first reading of the text, try to summarize it and answer your questions without looking back in the text. If you can't, you will need to reread all or part of the text. |
| Review | Once you have read the text, review it by looking through the text again to see what you remembered and reread sections that you have forgotten. |

5  Use close reading

Close reading strategies are mostly used in teacher-led direct instruction of difficult text. The hope, however, is that students will internalize close reading strategies and use them independently as well. There are many ways to teach students to read closely and carefully; in fact, SQ3R is a type of close reading. Below are the basic steps of a close reading lesson using challenging texts.

*Step 1: Pre-Reading*
– Carefully choose a complex but short text or section of text that will help students learn a standard-based content-focused learning target.
– Pre-read the text to determine essential vocabulary knowledge students will need and develop comprehension questions for the text.
– Pre-teach vocabulary and help students understand the purpose of the reading in connection with the learning target (for a review of learning targets, return to Chapter 4).
– Preview the text with students and help them build background knowledge.

*Step 2: First Reading*
– Have students read the text independently, in partners, or as a whole group.
– Ask them to ponder and talk about the main idea of the text.

*Step 3: Second Reading*
– Read the comprehension questions and restate the learning target.
– Reread the text with the comprehension questions and the learning target as the focus of the reading.
– Have students highlight or take notes on information related to the learning target and the questions.

*Step 4: Third Reading*
- Reread the text to fill in gaps in knowledge related to the learning target and comprehension questions.
- Think about how the text connects to previous learning targets or life experiences.

*Step 5: Post Reading*
- Write or discuss answers to the comprehension questions using direct textual evidence.

**Simple Tips, Hints, and Ideas for Using Leveled Texts**

Leveled texts can also be very helpful for learners. Below is one strategy for using them, as well as a list of places to find quality texts at all levels.

1 Individualized and all together thematic reading (IATT)

   Content-area learning targets and domain-specific reading skills can be gained in a way that is within the reach of readers at many levels. IATT provides reading experiences that are both individualized (by reading level) and cohesive to grade-level learning targets (focused on the same content-based themes). Sometimes struggling readers, especially when they are English language learners, do not get adequate experiences reading domain-specific texts (Haynes, 2015). This is a problem, because one of the main goals of content reading in school is for students to acquire the academic and domain language and literacy to succeed in future learning in the content area. Additionally, content reading allows students to be a part of the academic conversations surrounding the standards-based reading. When they aren't offered readable texts, gaps develop.

   The first step in IATT is to find leveled texts that fit your learning target. Sometimes it is challenging to find the perfect text at the perfect level for each student (though many great resources for leveled texts are shared below). That is why I sometimes use what I call *content-adjacent texts*. I wrote about it in a TESOL (Teaching English as a Second Language) blog:

   *If, for example, state science standards mandate and grade-level texts support learning about the process of the eclipse, students who read below the level of the textbook can read any book about the moon or sun.*

   (Platt & Wolfe, 2016)

   Even though the texts students read individually (or in small like-level groups of readers) are different and might be more content-adjacent than target-specific, they serve an important content-based learning experience in the "all together" portion of IATT.

Once students have completed reading, they move into the second step in IATT. This is when students come together in mixed groups to discuss what they read in relation to learning targets. No matter what text a reader used, he or she can contribute to the learning of the group as well as gain information from grade-level texts.

2 Resources for leveled (differentiated) texts
Below is a list of my favorite places to find quality differentiated reading materials. Gone are the days when teachers had to worry about their students feeling bad because they were reading what looked like a "baby book." There is a plethora of excellent leveled resources available.

- *Reading A to Z* (www.readinga-z.com) – Reading A to Z is a subscription service that costs about $110 per year. With a membership, teachers gain access to thousands of texts at a kindergarten through fifth grade reading level that can be downloaded, printed, and folded into books. There are many titles that have the same cover and information but are written at multiple levels so teachers can gear texts to students' individual reading levels. The nonfiction texts are excellent for middle grade students. Caution: The fiction texts, however, have not proven to be interesting or useful to my middle grade students.
- *Epic!* (www.getepic.com/) – This online reading platform continues to blow me away. It is free for educators and includes thousands of high-quality fiction and nonfiction books. Epic! works on iPads, Chromebooks, and the web. Most of the books are from first-rate publishers and are titles that I would love to be able to afford for my print library. There are also audiobooks and educational videos.
- *NewsELA* (https://newsela.com/) – NewsELA is a free website where teachers can create an online classroom and assign informational articles to students. Each text can be modified by Lexile (reading level), ranging from fourth to twelfth grade, by clicking on a slider. Many of the articles offered contain a short test, which is aligned to the Common Core State Standards-based tests.
- *TweenTribune* (www.tweentribune.com/) is similar to NewsELA.
- *ReadWorks* (www.readworks.org/) – This website offers hundreds of free short texts and fiction stories. That just-right text can easily be found using the sorting tools at the top of the resource page. Teachers can select for grade, Lexile level, subject, genre, skill, or strategy. Each reading passage comes with a carefully crafted question set.

- *Hi/Lo Books* (www.weteachwelearn.org/2015/07/highlow-books-to-engage-reluctant-readers-from-4th-grade-through-high-school/) – This is a list of my students' favorite hi/lo books. Hi/lo means high interest, low reading level. These texts tend to appeal to readers who struggle with grade-level texts but still want topics targeted to their age (including English learners). The idea is that if we give students books they *want* to read and *can* read, they *will* read them. Once readers finish one book, their confidence grows, and increased confidence can lead to increased reading. As any teacher knows, the more kids read, the better they read.
- *First Book* (www.fbmarketplace.org/) – Good leveled libraries must have lots and lots of books! Students should have the ability to choose books they want to read, and that means quantity matters. First Book Marketplace is an online store that offers high-quality, popular books at a fraction of the usual cost. You'll find a wide variety of books including nonfiction, novels, and picture books. Books with diverse characters are often featured.

### A Reminder: it's not an Either/or Thing

Use leveled texts all the time, some of the time, or none of the time. Great teachers come in all types and use diverse methods. As long as the focus is on helping students engage in effortful reading that helps them learn and grow and feel good about themselves, you're doing the right thing.

---

**Recapping the BIG Idea**

*Differentiated instruction is simply about helping each student move forward as a learner. It does not have to be fancy or time consuming for teachers.*

**In this chapter we looked at:**

1. Differentiated instruction in terms of content, process, environment, and product.
2. Offering students voice and choice in your classroom.
3. Allowing for differentiated texts in connection with your curriculum.

---

## References

Allington, R. (2002). You can't learn much from books you can't read. *Educational Leadership*, 60(3), 16–19.

Allington, R. (2013). What really matters when working with struggling readers. *The Reading Teacher*, 66(7), 520–530. doi:10.1002/trtr.1154

Dufour, R., Dufour, R., Eaker, R., & Many, T. (2006). *Learning by doing: A handbook for professional learning communities at work TM*. Bloomington, IN: Solution Tree.

DuFour, R., & Eaker, R. E. (2009). *Professional learning communities at work: Best practices for enhancing student achievement*. Moorabbin, Victoria: Hawker Brownlow Education.

Ferlazzo, L. (2018). *Differentiating instruction: It's not as hard as you think*. Retrieved from www.youtube.com/watch?v=h7-D3gi2lL8&feature=youtu.be

Glasswell, K., & Ford, M. (2010). *Teaching flexibly with leveled texts: More power for your reading block*. Retrieved from www.readingrockets.org/article/teaching-flexibly-leveled-texts-more-power-your-reading-block

Harris, A. J., & Sipay, E. R. (1990). *How to increase reading ability: A guide to developmental and remedial methods*. New York, NY: Longman.

Haynes, J. (2015). *Reading challenges for ELs in the age of the common core*. Retrieved from http://blog.tesol.org/reading-challenges-for-els-in-the-age-of-the-common-core/

Highfill, L., Hilton, K., & Landis, S. (2016). *The HyperDoc handbook: Digital lesson design using Google apps*. Irvine, CA: EdTechTeam Press.

Markle, B. (2018). *Reflections on shifting to a flexible classroom*. Retrieved from www.edutopia.org/article/reflections-shifting-flexible-classroom

National Education Association. (2017). *Reading wars*. Retrieved from www.nea.org/home/19392.htm

Platt, R., & Wolfe, J. (2016). *Content-adjacent reading focused teaching = content learning*. Retrieved from http://blog.tesol.org/content-adjacent-reading-focused-teaching-content-learning/

Popham, W. J. (2009). *Instruction that measures up: Successful teaching in the age of accountability*. Alexandria, VA: ASCD.

Shanahan, T. (2017). *New evidence on teaching reading at frustration levels*. Retrieved from http://www.readingrockets.org/blogs/shanahan-literacy/new-evidence-teaching-reading-frustration-levels

Shanahan, T. (2018). *How effective is independent reading in teaching reading?* Retrieved from http://shanahanonliteracy.com/blog/how-effective-is-independent-reading-in-teaching-reading#sthash.9Xmb7jIg.dpbs

Tomlinson, C. A. (2017). *How to differentiate instruction in academically diverse classrooms*. Moorabbin, VIC: Hawker Brownlow Education.

Tomlinson, C. A., & Moon, T. R. (2014). *Assessment and student success in a differentiated classroom*. Cheltenham, VIC: Hawker Brownlow Education.

Toshalis, E., & Nakkula, M. (2012). Motivation, engagement, and student choice. *Students at the Center*. Retrieved from www.howyouthlearn.org/pdf/Motivation Engagement Student Voice_0.pdf

# 6

# Social Animals

> **The BIG Idea**
>
> *Human beings are social animals. Teachers can harness the power of social proof and collaborative learning to engage students such that learning is joyful and students put forth maximum efforts.*
>
> **In this chapter you will:**
> 1. Read about social proof theory and how it connects to school-based learning.
> 2. Learn to focus students on examples of the academic work of their peers, older students, and members of the wider community.
> 3. Gain strategies to share academic learning inside of school and promote it outside of school with community members of all ages.
> 4. Plan to use collaborative learning and/or peer mentoring strategies and programs.

My daughter, a sixth grader at the local middle school, and I spend a lot of time together. The other day, we were chatting at the kitchen table and I asked her about her school day. Like many tweens, she shrugged and gave a noncommittal answer. I continued asking questions, "How was math? Anything new? What are you reading in language arts? Have you been on the climbing wall in gym?" Still nothing more than a one or two word answer.

Wanting to engage her in conversation, I asked about her favorite time of the school day: "Well, how about lunch, honey? Did you have a good lunch? Who did you hang out with?" Her reply broke my heart, "No, I don't have anyone to talk to at lunch; they are all on their phones or iPods texting each other."

When I said that seemed odd to me, "What? Why would they text each other when they are in the same room?" she said, "I don't know, Mom, but can I have an iPod?"

That conversation ended the same way they always do when one of my kids asks me for an electronic device.

No.

*"Kids today don't know how to communicate!"*
*"She has no social skills!"*
*"Teens don't talk to each other, they just text."*
*"He doesn't say hello or even make eye contact."*
*"They are always on their phones!"*

I will bet that you have heard these derisive comments about America's youth, or maybe you've even uttered them yourself. If I am totally honest, I have to admit that I have, and that's why, at least in part, my teen-aged son and tween-aged daughter do not have electronic devices at their disposal. Heck, we don't even have a television at our house.

Yes, it does seem that social skills are lacking when it comes to face-to-face communication. In fact, studies are increasingly confirming what some have been saying for a long time about the social cost of high tech. Read the quote below. Does it resonate with your experiences?

*For several millennia, humans' primary method for social learning and communication has been face to face. In the 21st century, as mobile technology and the Internet became available to most of the world's population, digital media have become an increasingly prevalent factor in the informal learning environment. Children today, ages 8–18, spend over 7½ hours a day, seven days a week using media outside of school. Moreover, teenagers, ages 12–17, report using phones to text message in their daily lives more than any other form of communication, including face-to-face socializing. The extensive time that children and teenagers engage with media and communicate using screens may be taking time away from face-to-face communication and some in-person activities.*

(Uhlsa, Michikyan, Morris, Garcia, Small, Zgourou, & Greenfield, 2014)

## 21st-century Skills

While the question of how much technology is too much continues to be discussed everywhere from my kitchen table to the offices of professors and

> **Your Turn!**
> - ★ Take a minute to think about what 21st-century or future-ready skills mean to you.
> - ★ Brainstorm a list.
> - ★ Are there other educators you know who might include different skills on the list?
> - ★ Look at the list below and compare it to your own.

research scientists in the hallowed halls of the best universities, a related topic is getting similar attention. That topic? 21st-century skills.

How many times have you heard the phrase "21st-century skills" in the last dozen years? Probably too many, although you may not hear it at all in some education circles. I was a librarian for many years, and my librarian friends refer to the skills as "future-ready" skills because, as they say (most of the time accompanied by a big eye roll), "We're already almost 20 years into the 21st century! How about we move into the future!"

Call them future-ready or 21st-century skills. Either way, it is important for teachers to define the skills if we are to incorporate them into our daily teaching.

Did your list contain a lot of technology-related concepts? I readily admit that mine did. But, really, technology use is just a part of what future-ready skills are all about.

The Partnership for 21st Century Learning offers a framework (2018) for understanding the skills. The framework shares a big-picture set of lists in four categories of skills and literacies that our students will likely need to be successful.

| Key Subjects and Themes Literacies | Learning and Innovation Skills | Information and Technology Skills Literacies | Life and Career Skills |
|---|---|---|---|
| • Global Awareness<br>• Financial<br>• Business<br>• Civic Literacy<br>• Health<br>• Environmental | • Creativity<br>• Critical Thinking<br>• Communication<br>• Collaboration | • Information<br>• Media<br>• Technology | • Flexibility<br>• Initiative<br>• Social<br>• Cross-Cultural<br>• Productivity<br>• Accountability<br>• Leadership |

> **Your Turn!**
> ★ Look at the skills and literacies lists on the previous page.
> ★ Highlight the skills that serve to help students be better communicators or that rely on communication skills.

No matter what list you consult or develop, communication is a critical aspect of preparing our students for whatever the future may hold for them. Teachers know that "a student who can't communicate effectively can't compete in the modern world. This is why teaching effective communication skills must serve as the cornerstone for any program preparing young people for the 21st century" (Wilczynski, 2009). Again, helping students master new technologies is part of good teaching for the future but not the be-all and end-all we sometimes hear it is.

## Students Learning from Students

We know that future-ready students must be good communicators. That means we must give them opportunities to practice communication skills by interacting with each other as a regular component of the learning experience. But that means more than using cooperative learning structures or strategies to increase direct student-to-student collaboration. We will talk about those later, I promise, but first, read about the incredible power of positive peer pressure through "social proof."

### Focusing the Message with Social Proof

Robert Cialdini (2006) writes about the idea that one of the best ways to influence people is to help them see something as socially normal. In other words, people tend to do what they see others doing. "Research on social proof has shown that our peers, in particular, and their choices are important to us and influence our decisions and actions. As a rule, we usually choose to do the same thing that our peers are doing" (Psychology Notes HQ, 2015).

The same is true when children see their entire community as supportive of an idea or an activity. When students see their peers and the wider community engaged in effortful learning, they see it as a social norm both inside and outside of school. According to social learning theory, once they see academic effort as the norm, they are more likely to work hard themselves.

After reading about the concept of social proof, I decided to leverage it in support of continuous and rigorous engagement in literacy activities. Most teachers are hopeful that their students will be more than just competent readers – we want them to be passionate readers. To this end, I wanted to help my students see the community engaged in reading and writing, to see literacy as a natural part of everyday life, not just a school thing.

**Simple Tips, Hints, and Ideas to Harness the Power of Social Proof**
Below are the strategies I use to build social proof. All were successful in part, I think, because each was equal parts challenging and fun.

1 Big read, little read
   The National Endowment for the Arts (NEA) promotes a community-wide read of a common novel, an experience called "The Big Read" (www.arts.gov/national-initiatives/nea-big-read). The novels are generally classics, and public libraries all over the country promote them through reading groups, discussion guides, and activity nights.
   For the past five years, I've partnered with my local public library to promote what we call "The Little Read." We choose a book that middle grade students can read, buy as many copies of it as we can, and ask community members and students to read it independently so we can later come together to talk about it. We have strong participation from both students and community members. Parents, retirees, school staff, school board members, and others all choose to read. As one participant once said, "The Big Read can be intimidating. I'm busy and don't have time for classics. But, with The Little Read, not only do I get to read a good book, but I also get to talk to young people. Win-win!" It is a win-win for me as well. Not only do I get kids reading and talking about books, but also I build positive public relations and goodwill in the community.
   I choose books that share themes and/or topics that mirror the Big Read choice. When the NEA's Big Read was *The Grapes of Wrath* by John Steinbeck, our Little Read was *Out of the Dust* by Karen Hesse. Both were set during the time of the Great Depression, which made it easy for cross-book discussions as well as those focused only on one book or the other.
   When the Big Read was *The Round House* by Louise Erdrich, the Little Read was the same author's *Chickadee*, another story of Ojibwe life, but written for students in grade 4 through high school. Last year, while the community at large read *Into the Beautiful North* by Luis Alberto Urrea, we read *Esperanza Rising* by Pam Muñoz Ryan.

> **Questions to Discuss**
> What was your favorite part?
> What characters did you most/least like?
> What themes popped out at you? What do you think the author wanted you to learn?

After everyone reads, we arrange for a picnic where students and community members talk about the book. The conversations are mostly organic, but I offer each group a list of possible starting points.

Engaging in The Little Read is a choice, and it is a choice that more than 100 students and community members make each year. It allows students to see that reading is something that adults who aren't teachers love to do, that reading is more than something people do as schoolwork.

2  Look who's reading!
This is a super simple idea. I ask students, families, and community members to take pictures (including selfies) of the reading they do outside of school. They text, message, email, or Facebook the pictures to me throughout the year, and I print them and post them on a prominent hallway bulletin board. Even better, perhaps, is that most often the pictures are shared with me through Facebook. My timeline is filled with pictures of kids reading and writing at home. In this way, the sharing itself provides social proof to the community. Caregivers start to think, "Huh. It looks like everyone's kids are reading at home. I better make sure mine are too!"

After I print and post the photos on the *real* wall (as opposed to the *virtual* one), I often catch students standing near the display of readers in action, talking about who they see and what they are reading. Last year I included pictures of folks writing too.

3  Reading friends
Reading Friends (Platt, 2015) is an intergenerational reading opportunity. My school's program pairs community members with reluctant or struggling readers. The adult friends, most of whom are retirees or stay-at-home parents, come to the school once a week to read with their student partners. Together they talk, read, laugh, and share thoughts about the books they're reading. The adult friends are encouraged to bring their books to the school to show students that they choose reading as a way to relax and enjoy life. The message seems to resonate with students, and they are beginning to see reading as a real-world activity.

4  Writer's conference
Once a year, I work with teachers and the wider community to facilitate a whole-day writer's conference for third graders. I invite local writers – including local newspaper reporters, published authors of books, poets, songwriters, bloggers, and journalists – to spend the day talking with

and teaching students about their lives as writers. The students dress up in professional clothes, attend a keynote speech, and enjoy concurrent sessions on topics from nonfiction writing to punching up dialogue in narrative works.

In the session I facilitate, I share my journals with students. They are amazed that I have written in them for over 30 years, and they love that I add sketches to the pages. All year, I troll Dollar Trees to find journals for each student, and I give each their own journal at the end of my session.

At the end of the conference, students fill out evaluations, and the feedback always includes students' joy to learn that they can write anytime they want outside of school.

5 Virtual visits

Skype, Google Hangouts, Zoom, Facetime, and other online communication systems allow global connections in amazingly quick and easy ways. Bringing authors, illustrators, scientists, artists, engineers, and others in to have virtual talks with your students is as easy as connecting to the internet.

Finding visitors is usually easy. Often, after students read a book they like, I will tweet or email the author, and more often than not, they get back to me and are willing to visit with my students! It really is amazing. The Skype in the Classroom site (https://education.microsoft.com/skype-in-the-classroom/overview) is a great place to find guests.

I have hosted dozens of Skype sessions for my students, and I am (and they are) rarely disappointed. As I shared in a blog post, "With each of these virtual visits, students made a connection with the world of reading and writing. In each case, they were inspired to read and write as a part of their own lives, engaging in hours of inspired thinking and creating" (Platt, 2017).

> **Your Turn!**
> ★ Think about your content area and how you could use the concept of social proof to enhance student learning.
> ★ Go to the Skype in the Classroom pages and look for visitors or virtual field trips you can bring to your students.

# Cooperative and Collaborative Learning

Collaboration is an important 21st-century (or future-ready, if you prefer) skill. Not only that, collaborative learning can help students work harder and have more fun!

Collaborative learning can be defined very simply as people working together to learn. In collaborative structures, students of various ages, grades, and proficiency levels might work in partners or groups where one student provides mentorship to others. Cooperative learning is a specific type of collaborative learning where all students are equal partners.

## Collaborative and Cooperative Learning in Practice

Before trying collaborative or cooperative learning, it is important to set students (and yourself) up for success. The best place to start is to lay a foundation for collaboration with a strong classroom climate of safety, mutual respect, and kindness (see Chapter 3 for a refresher). The next step is to be very intentional about developing student pairs and teams so that they are heterogeneous and primed for productive interaction.

John Strebe (2018) is an expert in collaborative learning methods. In his book, *Engaging Students Using Cooperative Learning*, he shares common mistakes made by teachers.

> *I have concluded that three major errors are responsible for less than satisfactory results in the interactive classroom.*
> - Team size was inappropriate for the class.
> - Team membership was not carefully, thoughtfully and purposefully decided.
> - Team building was not adequately done.
>
> (p. 13)

Cooperative learning guru Spencer Kagan (2011) recommends that in addition to careful selection of cooperative partners or groups and a strong positive classroom climate, teachers should plan for cooperative learning with PIES. He claims,

> *If any of the four PIES principles is left out, the interaction is group work, not cooperative learning. For us PIES are what defines cooperative learning . . . when we have our students do group work, we do not take responsibility for structuring for the equality. We hope it happens, but do not make it happen. I am fond of saying group work is wishful thinking.*
>
> (Kagan, 2011)

| **P**ositive Interdependence | <ul><li>All students must work together to be successful.</li><li>Each student must count on the others.</li><li>Each student must contribute.</li><li>"Positive interdependence drives cooperation. When our outcomes are linked, we hope for and support the success of others; when we cannot do a task alone, we work with others" (Kagan, 2011).</li></ul> |
|---|---|
| **I**ndividual Accountability | <ul><li>If teachers want to have optimal learning come from collaborative work, each student must participate.</li><li>No student can "hide" from learning and practice.</li><li>Each student must participate in some form of individual assessment.</li><li>"Individual accountability drives achievement. When we know we will be held accountable for an individual performance, we are more motivated and try harder than when we know no one will see how much we have learned or how well we can perform" (Kagan, 2011).</li></ul> |
| **E**qual Participation | <ul><li>Every student must participate.</li><li>Tasks are designed to engage all learners.</li><li>All students are equally important to learning.</li><li>"Students learn by interacting with the content and with fellow students so participation must be relatively equal" (Kagan & Kagan, 2009, p. 12).</li></ul> |
| **S**imultaneous Interaction | <ul><li>All students are actively engaged nearly 100% of the time.</li><li>Students talk, share, and seek to work together to accomplish a learning task.</li></ul> |

### Simple Tips, Hints, and Ideas for Using Collaborative and Cooperative Learning

There are probably as many strategies for collaborative and cooperative learning as there are teachers. Some are as simple as having students practice partner reading (see Chapter 5) while others require more involved planning and monitoring. Below are some of my favorite and successful tips, hints, and ideas for using collaborative learning in your classroom.

1 Cross-age tutoring
   My favorite half hour of the day is the time when I supervise my all-volunteer army of fourth graders (whom I call the "bigs") as they

work one on one with first graders ("littles") who need a boost in reading proficiency. It is a cross-age tutoring delight!

As a part of our Tier II reading intervention program (RTI), the bigs give up their lunch recess to mentor the littles. I train the fourth graders during "working lunches" and offer them a tight schedule of activities to complete with their students.

Listening to the productive buzz of kids helping kids, watching the bigs as they gently and kindly encourage their partners, and seeing the admiration in the eyes of the littles as they beam under the praise from their mentors is truly a wonder. The academic benefits are many, but the social-emotional bonuses might supersede them. Remember the power of "social proof"? The young students in my program get a good dose of it from their tutors every day; they recognize that the bigs are "into" reading and writing and, as such, that literacy is cool.

## 2 Kagan strategies

You are likely familiar with Kagan's name from the section above that included PIES. Kagan (Kagan & Kagan, 2009) has designed many easy-to-implement strategies to help students work in cooperative learning groups. Below, you will read about four.

- *Quiz-Quiz-Trade*. To use quiz-quiz-trade, write several questions or problems that help students think about a topic, vocabulary words, or a concept. Write the questions or problems on index cards with the answer on the opposite side. Each student gets a card. All students find a partner and one quizzes the other. If their partner is correct, they provide praise; if not, they provide their partner with encouragement and share the correct answer. Then roles are switched. When both partners have had a turn, they trade cards and trade partners. The classroom is sure to be loud and active, and learning is almost guaranteed. I love to use this method for test review, math facts or problem practice, and vocabulary.
- *Numbered Heads Together*. This is a simple cooperative structure that can be used across curriculum and with students of all ages. The teacher places students in groups of four and gives each student a number (from 1 to 4). The teacher asks a question or gives students a topic for discussion. Students lean in to discuss, making sure that everyone on the team can answer the question and fully comprehends the answer. The teacher then calls out a number from one to four and the student who corresponds to it writes or speaks the answer on behalf of the group. This is a great structure for both quick and longer discussions. It virtually ensures that all students talk.

- *Rally Coach*. This strategy pairs students where one is labeled "A" and the other "B." Once the teacher has assigned a task, both students independently complete it. This may be a worksheet, a written assignment, a graphic organizer, a math problem, or any other written task. Once Student A and Student B finish, they take turns coaching one another. Student A checks and discusses Student B's work and then vice versa. I love this strategy for math problems, short written answers, and simple project-based learning.
- *Give One, Get One*. A great strategy for helping students share prior knowledge or review content, Give One, Get One calls on students to share ideas and information. Have students draw a table with two columns and as many rows as are needed. Give students a topic and have them fill in one row with known information. Then, set students loose in the room to share (give one) what they know with others and to learn new information about the topic (get one) from a classmate with the caveat that students must find a new person each time they give one and get one.
- *Think, Pair, Share (TPS)*. This strategy offers students the chance for structured interaction. The idea is to offer a prompt, most often in the form of a question, and ask students to interact with it in three steps. First, give time for students to think. Second, allow students to pair and talk about their thoughts and ideas. Third, ask students to share with another pair or with the whole group. To make TPS work optimally, it is important to offer think time, to insist that all students interact, and to monitor their talk to make sure it is substantive. While TPS is often used, in my experience, it is not often used as well as it could be. Look at the chart and example below for ideas on how to incorporate TPS effectively.

| **Think** | **Pair** | **Share** |
|---|---|---|
| **Students can independently think in a variety of ways at the time it makes most sense.**<br>• Silently<br>• In writing<br>• As a drawing<br>• Before class begins<br>• During the lesson | **Students can think with a partner in a variety of ways.**<br><br>• Talk about thoughts<br>• Read each other's thoughts<br>• Make arguments<br>• Find support<br>• During the lesson | **Students can share with the group in a variety of ways at the time it makes the most sense.**<br>• With another pair<br>• Whole group<br>• Through polling software<br>• On a Google Doc<br>• In a written format<br>• During the lesson<br>• The next day |

Example:

*Ms. Renraw is teaching a lesson on how animals adapt to their environment. Her students have studied several examples, and she wants them to generalize the information to other animals. She decides to use TPS as the method.*

*She says, "Students, we've looked at how owls, worms, and fennec foxes have adapted to their different environments. I'd like to see if you can look at three other animals and think about what features they have that illustrate how well they are well adapted to their environment. Please look at these photos."*

*Ms. Renraw shows students pictures of a hummingbird, a rattlesnake, and a rat and asks students to take three minutes to silently **think** about the adaptations they see in each. After three minutes, she numbers students as a one, two, or three (each number corresponding to the hummingbird, rattlesnake, and rat respectively). She says, "Now, you're going to **think** again. Take three minutes to write down all of the adaptations you see or know about in the animal assigned to you."*

After three minutes, she instructs students to find a partner to **pair** with and says, "Please talk through your list with a partner. Take turns and listen to each other. Combine your lists." As students do this work, Ms. Renraw circulates and listens. When she sees students off-task, she politely redirects them.

When students are finished, Ms. Renraw moves them to the **share** portion of the TPS experience. She says, "Please group in sets of three pairs to share. Each group should have a pair that discussed hummingbirds, rattlesnakes, and rats. Take turns sharing in the wider group. Please help each other and add to each other's lists if you can."

Again, she circulates and monitors student discussion. When students have finished, she offers them directions to help them **share** at the next level. She says, "Please go back to your original partner and create a Google Slide for the information. Students in all of my classes will have access to all of the slides. Tomorrow, you will see how what you came up with is similar to and different from groups in other periods."

3 Collaborative worksheets, reviews, and lectures

Collaboration can even happen during what is typically thought of as old-school learning. Lectures and worksheets do not need to be silent or (here comes a word most teachers and all parents despise) boring. Use the strategies below to get students working together during more traditional methods of instruction.
- *RDC.* This strategy is in many ways similar to TPS. Students work together in pairs to learn information, ideas, or strategies presented on a worksheet. They use the RDC model. **R**espect: students have time to independently and silently read through, think about the

material provided, and write down answers. **Defense:** Students work with their partner to defend and justify any conclusions they made about the content or answers they've written on the worksheet. **Consensus:** Paired students meet with another pair to come to consensus about the information on the worksheet. When no consensus can be found, students work with a teacher to clarify the information (Strebe, 2018).

– *Think, Pair, Square, Share*. Using another modification of TPS, there is even room for collaborative learning as a part of a lecture through the *think/pair/square/share* strategy for making lectures interactive. In this strategy, the teacher preplans stopping points to ask students questions during a lecture. When the teacher asks a question, students think about it in four modes. **T**hink allows for silent independent thought, **P**air offers students the chance to discuss thoughts with a partner, **S**quare enlarges the discussion to a group of four (two established pairs combined), and **S**hare is when square teams offer the answer to the teacher or the entire class (Strebe, 2018).

– *My Mistake*. This strategy works best with worksheets that are designed to review learning. Students complete the worksheet independently but make one or more (the teacher should give an exact

---

**Your Turn!**

★ Review the collaborative strategies above and think about how you could use each.
1. Cross-Age Tutoring
2. Kagan Strategies
   - Quiz-Quiz-Trade
   - Numbered Heads Together
   - Rally Coach
   - Give One, Get One
   - TPS
3. Collaborative Worksheets
   - RDC
   - Think, Pair, Square, Share
   - My Mistake

★ Choose one of the strategies to try with your students and reflect on what went well and what you might need to tweak to make it work for your class.

number) intentional mistakes. Then, students trade papers with a partner and look for and correct the mistakes. Once mistakes are corrected, students work with their partners to discuss each mistake. When mistakes cannot be found or there is disagreement, the teacher shares the example with the entire group for discussion (Watson, 2016).

### Classroom Management – a Quick Review

It is important to remember that a loud or active classroom does not necessarily equal one that is out of control. However, as previously shared in Chapter 3, strong classroom management is the bottom line in effective teaching. I am not dogmatic about what style of classroom management is best – there are many effective methods to keep a class productively humming.

Methods and personal styles allow classroom management to manifest in myriad ways. The important thing is that using collaborative learning strategies doesn't result in a class becoming "out of control." Remember, a classroom that is "in control" is one where students are focused and learning occurs. When your students are engaged in cooperative learning, make sure you can answer yes to the following questions. If you can't, don't abandon collaborative strategies; problem-solve and work with your students to employ the strategies more effectively.

In my classroom,

- ◆ am I and are my students happy and relaxed?
- ◆ is learning the focus rather than non-learning-focused socializing?
- ◆ are students able to articulate the learning targets they are collaboratively working toward meeting?
- ◆ do students make demonstrable growth in the content I teach?

### We Need Each Other!

I had the good fortune of listening to Professor Gloria Ladsen-Billings speak recently. In Chapter 3 of this book, I shared a little bit about her work with the concept of culturally relevant teaching. In listening to her speak, I found one theme arose again and again: the idea that children are inherently social. It is normal and right that they want to talk to each other. Instead of stifling interactions, the teacher can and should use that desire to hear and be heard as a part of the learning process.

In Laden-Billings' seminal 1995 article, *Toward a Theory of Culturally Relevant Pedagogy*, she examined the qualities of teachers who offered students of color exemplary educations. I think you'll agree that her words are easily extrapolated to teachers who are successful with students of most backgrounds.

> *To solidify the social relationships in their classes, the teachers encouraged the students to learn collaboratively, teach each other, and be responsible for the academic success of others. These collaborative arrangements were not necessarily structured like those of cooperative learning. Instead, the teachers used a combination of formal and informal peer collaborations. One teacher used a buddy system, where each student was paired with another. The buddies checked each other's homework and class assignments. Buddies quizzed each other for tests, and, if one buddy was absent, it was the responsibility of the other to call to see why and to help with makeup work. The teachers used this ethos of reciprocity and mutuality to insist that one person's success was the success of all and one person's failure was the failure of all. These feelings were exemplified by the teacher who insisted, "We're a family. We have to care for one another as if our very survival depended on it. . . . Actually, it does!"*
>
> (Ladson-Billings, 1995)

---

**Recapping the BIG Idea**

*Human beings are social animals. Teachers can harness the power of social proof and collaborative learning to engage students such that learning is joyful and students put forth maximum efforts.*

In this chapter we looked at:

1. Social proof theory and how it connects to school-based learning.
2. Using examples of the academic work of your students' peers, older students, and members of the wider community to build a strong culture of learning.
3. Strategies to share academic learning inside of school and promote it outside of school with the wider community.
4. Collaborative learning and/or peer mentoring strategies and programs.

---

## References

Cialdini, R. B. (2006). *Influence: The psychology of persuasion*. New York, NY: Collins.

Framework for 21st Century Learning. (2018). Retrieved from www.p21.org/our-work/p21-framework

Kagan, S. (2011). *The "P" and "I" of PIES: Powerful principles for success.* San Clemente, CA: Kagan Publishing. *Kagan Online Magazine,* Fall/Winter. Retrieved from https://www.kaganonline.com/free_articles/dr_spencer_kagan/345/The-P-and-I-of-PIES-Powerful-Principles-for-Success.

Kagan, S., & Kagan, M. (2009). *Kagan cooperative learning.* San Clemente, CA: Kagan Publishing.

Ladson-Billings, G. (1995). Toward a theory of culturally relevant pedagogy. *American Educational Research Journal, 32*(3), 465. doi:10.2307/1163320

Platt, R. (2017). *Bringing authors into your classroom.* Retrieved from www.edutopia.org/blog/bringing-authors-classroom-rita-platt

Platt, R. (2015). *Reading friends tutoring.* Retrieved from www.programminglibrarian.org/programs/reading-friends-tutoring

Psychology Notes HQ. (2015). *What is the social proof theory?* Retrieved from www.psychologynoteshq.com/social-proof/

Strebe, J. D. (2018). *Engaging students using cooperative learning.* New York, NY: Routledge.

Uhlsa, Y., Michikyan, M., Morris, J., Garcia, D., Small, G., Zgourou, E., & Greenfield, P. (2014). *Five days at outdoor education camp without screens improves preteen skills with nonverbal emotion cues.* Retrieved from www.sciencedirect.com/science/article/pii/S0747563214003227

Watson, A. (2016). *5 ways to turn a worksheet into a collaborative critical-thinking activity.* Retrieved from https://thecornerstoneforteachers.com/worksheet/

Wilczynski, E. (2009). *Teaching basic communication skills.* Retrieved from www.seenmagazine.us/Articles/Article-Detail/ArticleId/209/Teaching-Basic-Communication-Skills

# 7

# Busting Down the Walls, Building Community Connections

> **The BIG Idea**
> *When students' home lives are connected with their school lives, they are more likely to work hard and be happy.*
>
> **In this chapter you will:**
> 1. Read about how being connected with the communities of your students can help make for a harmonious classroom experience for teachers and students alike.
> 2. Think about the types of caregiver involvement and how you can value them.
> 3. Learn how to use social media and cell phones to reach out to the families of your students in simple but frequent ways.
> 4. Explore ideas for being present in the community you serve.

Building strong relationships has always been important to me. From my perspective, when educators know the community of the school in general and the families and caregivers of the students they serve in specific, magic can happen. That magic serves to foster both effort and joy in the classroom.

In Chapter 3, you read about building relationships with students. Many of those same strategies can be applied to community relationships. This chapter seeks to take a closer look at how to intentionally break down walls that sometimes separate educators from the communities in which they seek to make a difference.

When I first took on the role as the principal of my school, among my immediate priorities was to repair relationships that seemed negative and to cultivate new and very positive relationships. To that end, I reached out with a renewed vigor. I have always been actively engaged in community life, attending events, volunteering, serving on committees, and the like, but I wanted to make that engagement more personal.

I started very simply, by "friending" many of the moms, dads, and other caregivers of the kids at my school on Facebook. That led to invitations to birthday parties, one-on-one conversations, and other community events and thus to an immense amount of information about the home lives of my students. It mattered. Read the comments below to see how much.

- *Thank you for listening. I just felt like no one ever listened to me.*
- *Thank you for coming. It means so much. You mean the world to my girls and me.*
- *You have restored my faith in public education.*
- *I so appreciate you – always willing to help and reach out. Sincerely grateful for you. Thanks for being so good to us and loving [my daughter] so much.*

## Why Bother?

As noted above, it doesn't take a deep dive into the research to understand how important it is to have strong relationships with the families and caregivers of the students you serve. That said, the research on engagement, particularly caregiver involvement, is interesting in part because it doesn't say what many of us think it does.

A return to John Hattie's (2009) meta-analysis reveals that parental involvement has a high positive effect strength and is strongly related to increased student achievement. The data shows that it behooves schools and families to work as partners when it comes to student achievement. Yes, okay, I know, I can almost see readers rolling their eyes at this. Of course students do better when their caregivers are involved in their school lives. Again, however, involvement can manifest itself in a variety of "non-traditional" ways. Take the quiz below to test your own knowledge of what matters most in terms of student engagement. Read each statement and decide how important it is to academic achievement. Then assign it a score from 1 to 3 (with 3 being very important, 2 being somewhat important, and 1 being not important).

|   | **Example of Caregiver Involvement or Engagement** | **How Important is it?** |
|---|---|---|
| 1 | Offering verbal support of schools. | |
| 2 | Showing up at school events. | |
| 3 | Volunteering at the school during the day or in a parent group. | |
| 4 | Encouraging home reading. | |
| 5 | Discussing day-to-day life and learning with children. | |
| 6 | Checking grades on web-based gradebooks. | |
| 7 | Punishing students at home for misbehavior at school. | |

For the most part, any of the above could be helpful to student achievement if used well, and some are more strongly supported by Hattie's research than others are. For example, numbers 4, 5, and 7 have a much stronger positive effect strength than 2 and 6 have.

What might come as a big surprise to some is that number 1, offering verbal support of schools, has the highest potential for positive impact. Even more surprising? Not only does number 6, checking grades on web-based gradebooks, not work to increase student achievement, it often backfires entirely and reduces a student's chances for increased academic success (Lahey, 2017). Lahey writes, "When we focus our attention on real-time, up-to-the-second reporting on the portal, we elevate the false idols of scores and grades and devalue what really has an impact on learning: positive student-teacher relationships, relevance and student engagement."

## Involvement Versus Engagement of Caregivers

Teacher, writer, and prominent education blogger Larry Ferlazzo (2011) explains that there is a difference between the word *involvement* and the word *engagement* and says that educators should set their sights on engagement rather than involvement. Engagement, shares Ferlazzo, is more encompassing, more indicative of partnership, and more realistic than the idea of involvement. Additionally, he cautions against thinking about caregiver involvement rather than engagement because of the baggage that comes with the sense that parents aren't involved enough. Go to any staff lounge in the country and sooner or later you'll hear teachers complaining that parents aren't involved enough. It might even be true. But, as Ferlazzo says, we should be more focused on engagement anyway.

Involvement happens when schools do most of the talking and think about caregivers as less than full partners in their children's education. Caregiver involvement activities are marked by an absence of the caregiver in the decision-making, planning, and execution of activities.

For example, asking parents to sign paperwork, attend family nights, and read newsletters are all examples of what is typically labeled caregiver involvement. Engagement, on the other hand, means recognizing that parents have a voice by asking them to share their wants and needs for their child.

Another example can be highlighted in terms of communication style. Involvement is characterized by one-way communication. Teachers might expect that parents check into an electronic gradebook as the main avenue for communication, or a teacher might send letters or notes to homes but is not necessarily available to chat and/or cannot be reached by phone, text, or social media. Engagement, on the other hand, might happen when the teacher sets up regular meetings, provides ample opportunities to have two-way discussions, and provides multiple ways to reach him or her.

A healthy balance of involvement and engagement is probably the winning idea. No matter what, we must all be careful to monitor our assumptions. Even if caregivers are not as "involved" or "engaged" as we might want them to be, we must remember that the vast majority of parents still care. The chart below describes the different types of caregiver interaction. Which do you think connote caregiver engagement?

## A Framework for Caregiver Engagement

Joyce Epstein (1995) developed a framework for thinking about caregiver interaction, which revolves around six basic types.

| Type | Characteristics/Examples |
| --- | --- |
| Supportive | • Talks with student about the importance of school.<br>• Supports school rules.<br>• Helps with homework and organization. |
| Communicative | • Returns paperwork.<br>• Responds to calls and texts.<br>• Interacts with social media.<br>• Reaches out to school to communicate. |
| Attends | • Comes to conferences.<br>• Comes into the school for planned activities.<br>• Attends sports events. |

| Type | Characteristics/Examples |
|---|---|
| Volunteers | • Helps in the classroom.<br>• Chaperones field trips, parties, and other events.<br>• Does guest presentations (shares expertise with students). |
| Advocates | • Volunteers with parent groups (for example, PTA).<br>• Hosts after-school clubs or coaches teams.<br>• Raises funds.<br>• Serves on committees. |
| Parents (as a verb) | • Helps child get enough sleep and eat healthy meals.<br>• Encourages responsibility.<br>• Ensures child gets to school on time. |

There has been some criticism of Epstein's work, suggesting it does not adequately acknowledge the power differential that often favors the school's view of engagement over that of families (Green, 2013). There is, of course, truth to the critique. However, when used as an avenue to address all of the ways that students' caregivers are involved in their learning (without assigning any value judgments), Epstein's framework can indeed provide proof that caregivers do in fact care and are involved and engaged in their children's educational journey.

## Positive Phone Calls and Social Media Sharing

A great way to build connections and knock down walls between the school and the community is to communicate through phone calls and social media.

### Reach Out and Touch Someone!

How many times have you tried calling a caregiver, only to find that s/he won't answer? It shouldn't surprise you. So often, the calls caregivers receive from schools are negative. We call to ask for help with poor behavior. We call

> **Your Turn!**
> ★ Review the types of engagement in the chart above. Reflect on what resonates with your experience as an educator or a caregiver. Ask yourself the types of involvement/engagement you'd like to begin to foster.

when homework is not done. We call to remind. We sometimes even call to scold.

It's time to flip that dynamic and call parents when kids do something good! Making positive phone calls takes time, but it is worth every minute spent and it doesn't have to be done in one day, one week, or even one month.

Make it a goal to call or text two to five families a week to share a kind word about their children (your students). Observe your kiddos as they work and play and jot down any positives you notice.

- Does the student have a nice smile?
- Did someone get to class right on time or always come prepared?
- Did a student ask a good question?
- Did you catch one of your students helping a classmate?
- Did the student finish an assignment on time?
- Did a youngster earn an "A" on a difficult project?
- Did someone make great growth on an assessment?
- Did one of your readers finish a challenging book?
- Did a kid tell you a funny story?

Once you have something specific and positive to share, start by calling the caregivers of students who may have had phone calls home in the past for doing something wrong. Make sure you tell the students when you call or text their parents. You may be surprised to learn how much it means, to even your seemingly toughest kids, to learn that you care enough to call with positive news.

I make it a habit to carry my cell phone in my pocket. I try to call at least two families per week right in front of my students. If someone does something great, I'll pull out my phone and ask the kid to dial his mom or dad's number. Then, right in front of everyone, I will sing his praises. The students love it and all ask if I can call their mom or dad next! It is really motivating. I get lots of return calls and emails from parents telling me how happy it made them.

An added benefit of calling to share good news is that if or when you need to call to ask for support, to remind, or to share a negative consequence a student has earned, parents are more likely to answer the phone and listen to you. Positive phone calls breed positive feelings. I think that caregivers are more receptive to me because the phone calls help them to know I care. It is totally worth the extra effort in the long run.

If you are interested in trying positive phone calls, but are unsure of what to say, try using the script that follows or writing your own prompt. If you get voice mail, no problem, leave an upbeat message with instructions for how to reach you.

---

**Phone Script 1**

Hello Ms._____. This is Ms. _____ calling to share good news about your son! This week he was in class on time every day and really participated well in class! I am so happy to have him as a student. Please feel free to call me anytime. I love working with families.

**Phone Script 2**

Hi, this is Mr. _____ calling to tell you how much I enjoy having your daughter in my class! This week she volunteered to read aloud from the textbook and I was so impressed with her bravery. Thank you for letting me work with her this year. Let me know if there is ever anything I can help you with.

**Phone Script 3**

Hello Ms. _____. This is Mrs. _____ calling to tell you that _____ earned an "A" on her assignment this week! She is so proud of herself and she should be! Thank you! You clearly have taught her to value education. Please feel free to call me anytime! Take care!

---

If you can't call for one reason or another, email, text, or message parents with positive information. In fact, many caregivers prefer text to phone messages. They serve the same purpose and for those who don't like phone calls, an e-message might even be better.

## Social Media Sharing

In my neck of the woods, people are on Facebook, which means so am I, and I am one thumbs-upping gal. I post pictures, make short videos, and ask questions. I also take a few minutes each day to look at what others post and "like" and comment. Because of Facebook, I am able to ask students about how that trip to Yellowstone was or how their sick uncle is feeling. Folks put their life out on Facebook, and I am grateful for the ways in which it helps me

---

**Your Turn!**
- ★ Set a goal for how many positive phone calls or contacts you will make each week.
- ★ Get started right now! Put down this book, pick up your phone, and make that positive call!

connect. It is amazing how big an impact a social media presence can have. Families are comfortable with me and I am comfortable with them.

These days Facebook, Twitter, Snapchat, Instagram, and other social media networks are among the most common ways that people communicate with one another. In many ways, I think of Facebook (again, what folks in my town tend to use) as the town square or community meeting place. I love to travel and have spent quite a bit of time in Asia. Over and over again, while there, I noticed that in villages, towns, cities, and megalopolises alike, once the workday is done, families join together in community spaces to eat picnics, watch children play, laugh, dance, and talk. Social media is as close to that as many towns come these days. It may not be exactly the same, but it's good and there may not be a better way to break down walls and open the lines of communication with caregivers than by using social media as a tool.

If you do choose to use social media, there are some guidelines to follow.

1. Check your school and district policy on social media and make sure having a class account is okay.
2. Make a separate account for school purposes only that is not tied to your personal account. The school account is the one where you are safe to "friend" students and parents. Consider making a group as well. Groups can be closed and only parents you invite or those who ask to join can view the site.
3. Keep all comments professional and about topics of teaching and learning. Contrary to some teachers' beliefs, there are limits to free speech when it comes to engaging with the community. An increasing number of teachers are facing legal actions as a result of defamatory statements posted online about schools, districts, students, and parents.
4. Do not post pictures of students without written caregiver approval. With your principal's permission, you can send home a consent form for parents to sign.
5. Remove students' names before posting their work.

### Simple Tips, Hints, and Ideas to Communicate with Caregivers

So far everything shared in this chapter is done with an eye toward improved communication. Walls cannot come down until there is trust and understanding, and the root of both of those is in effortful and joyous communication between schools and the wider school community, including the caregivers of our students. Below are three simple tips that can be applied widely and fairly easily.

1  Be transparent!
   One of the reasons that parents are not involved or engaged is that they do not have a solid grasp of school or teacher expectations. If you want caregivers engaged, you have to give a little to get a little! Make your expectations and the happenings at your school clear and easy to access. This can be done on social media, but occasionally sending written notes home can be helpful too. Of course, at the middle school, junior high, and high school level weekly notes or letters are not always an ideal way to communicate. Think about it. If a student has seven classes, that means seven weekly letters going home! How many are likely to be read? However, if all teachers get together on a shared document (think Google Docs or Word Online) where each shared a brief summary of class happenings that week, many caregivers would appreciate it.

   My own children's teachers share a joint weekly email with caregivers, and I am grateful to have a sense of what my kids are learning so that when I say, "What's going on at school" and they say, "Nothing," I will have a wedge to get the conversation going by saying, "Aren't you working on learning decimal conversions in math? How's that going?"

   That said, writing a good quarterly or once-a-semester handbook of sorts can be very helpful to parents, students, and teachers alike. Below are some things to consider including in the letter.
   – Contact information
   – Grading policy
   – Learning targets
   – Homework expectations
   – Discipline policy
   Keep it friendly. Think of this as a kind of School User's Manual for caregivers.

2  Judge less, love more
   "If you judge people, you have no time to love them." This quote, attributed to Mother Teresa, is one of my all-time favorites. If we are to truly break down walls in ways that allow us to open to others and build strong relationships, we have to cast judgment aside. I have a mentor, former principal Irene Brenner, who always says something similar. To paraphrase, she says, *"Every parent is doing the best they can. Treat them with respect and that will be reflected back at you"*.

3  Look approachable!
   Take off the tie and/or the high heels. Unless you live in a community where everyone is dressed to the nines, or it is your own preferred style of dress, take it down a notch. One of the teachers on my staff recently

asked me if it was okay to wear jeans to school. My reply was, that short of athletic wear (sweats, in particular), as long as she looked neat, fresh, and put together, jeans are fine. Our school is in rural Wisconsin and most folks dress casually. While I don't want my teachers to dress in flannels and Carhartt work bibs, I also don't want them to dress in a way that puts a wedge between school personnel and the community we serve.

4  Watch out for RBF and smile, smile, smile!
*Smile at people and make eye contact*. Every time. Don't pass people in the hallways or outside without a simple acknowledgement. A smile, a head nod, or a wave is a small gesture, but it makes a big difference. These days there is a common meme about folks who don't smile a lot. The joke is that they have what's called RBF Syndrome (see the quote in the box and if you still don't get what RBF stands for, look it up, I'm not going to say it out loud!). Now, for full disclosure, I don't have RBF. In fact, my husband once commented, "Rita, I love that a smile is your default facial expression!" While it was one of the nicest compliments I've ever had, I know that it has less to do with my attitude than it does my DNA. I was born smiling and tend toward a Pollyanna-esque outlook. Not everyone runs around looking like a smiley-face emoji and that's fine. But a personal greeting and/or a quick smile can go a long way. Being cognizant of that is important and sets the foundation for good relationships with your larger school community.

> **"I'm Not** Angry, This is Just my face"

## Be Visible!

A big part of connecting with students and their families is just being present in the community. Just seeing and being seen. In the early 2000s, I taught in remote Yupik and Inupiat villages on the Bering Sea Coast of Alaska. The villages were accessible only by airplane, and the residents ranged from the school-aged children I served to elders who spoke no English and had never travelled further than a mile or two outside of their town. My first year in this unique environment, I was lucky to have a mentor who told me the following story.

> *Years ago, I learned a valuable lesson about what it means to be seen in the village. I lived on the other side of the beach across the village from school. So every day I walked the half-mile lane from my house to work. When the district built new teacher housing, right next door to my classroom, I moved in. Not long after, I was at the town hall at a community dance and an elder*

*approached me. She only spoke Yupik and I only spoke English, so we communicated through her granddaughter, who was my student.*

*"She wants to know why you never visit her anymore," my student translated. I was confused, I had never visited her house, I thought maybe she had me mixed up with another teacher, most of whom were not Yupik. My student clarified, saying, "She means when you used to walk by her house every day. She wants to know if you don't like seeing her anymore." I realized that to her, just seeing me walk through town mattered very much. She felt she knew me and that I knew her.*

I have often thought of that story and have used it as a reminder that being *in the community* is important. To that end, I try to do regular business in the same neighborhood where I teach. I have to go to the bank, fill up the car, walk the dog, and grocery shop, right? Why not do it where the students and families I serve are doing those things too? The more the community sees you, the more likely community members are to reach out to you and to be open when you reach out to them.

**Simple Tips, Hints, and Ideas to be Present in your Students' Communities**

In addition to just doing your regular business in the community where you teach, below are some easy ways to involve yourself in the community.

1 More on meetups...
   In Chapter 3, you read about how I often organize simple "meetups" with my students and the community. If you remember, I will put out a notice on Facebook about where I'll be and when I'll be there, and then whoever shows up, shows up! The examples from Chapter 3 included meetings at the public library and a community public concert. Arranging meetups at local parks, at pickup games of baseball at the local diamond, or at the movie theater are also great ways to connect.

   The best family night I ever had was a meetup where I asked parents to come to a local park after school hours and share a meal together. There was no formal talk about schedules or school rules. I didn't make a big presentation. Everyone brought a dish to share and I ordered a few pizzas just in case. The kids sat in small groups together and so did the parents. We all introduced ourselves after dinner and played a game of get-to-know-you bingo. Many new friendships were formed. I brought my own husband and children and I felt like parents and students viewed me as a whole person rather than just a teacher who lives in the school, as some certainly thought before that night! It really helped build community and positive culture that lasted all year in my room.

2  Get your sports on!

Going to students' games means a lot. While I am in no way, shape, or form a sports fan and can barely tell the difference between the various "sports games," as I like to call them, I go to them. Seeing my students at the high school football stadium as they cheer on the team or watching them in their softball tournaments is a great way to see kids in the community. Because I really don't care much for sports as entertainment, I often volunteer to work the concessions stand. That way, I get to greet my students and their families and feel like a productive member of the community without actually having to watch the game.

3  Home visits

I freely admit, this one's not for everyone. Years ago, when I lived in rural Alaska, I would home visit each of my students a couple of times a year, but over the years home visits have drifted out of my practice. Then I read *Lead Like a Pirate* (Burgess & Houf, 2017) and was inspired by middle school principal Beth Houf. Houf and her assistant principal, or "cocaptain" as she says, do home visits for each of their incoming sixth grade students. That floored me and made me want to do more to connect with my own families.

Gradually, I've added home visits back into my life as an educator. I have visited the homes of many students, but particularly those whom I have had trouble connecting with for one reason or another. It is been helpful, fun, and profoundly interesting.

If you are interested in trying a home visit or two, there are general guidelines that might prove helpful (Teaching Tolerance, 2017).

- Always schedule home visits; never show up unannounced.
- Go with a partner (I admit, I tend to go alone, but I teach in a small town and feel safe).
- Bring a translator if one is needed.
- Keep the visit from between 15 to 30 minutes.
- Be positive and keep the conversation light. Think of one or two nice things to say about your student to her/his family. Do not talk about grades or poor behavior.

Additionally, I have had many children to my own house (which is only a block from the school). Students have come over to check out my rock garden as a part of science class and to celebrate meeting goals. All in all, hundreds of kids have come to my house this year, and it has helped deepen my connections with each of them and helped their families see me as a part of the community.

> **Recapping the BIG Idea**
>
> ***When students' home lives are connected with their school lives, they are more likely to work hard and be happy.***
>
> **In this chapter we looked at:**
>
> 1. How being connected with the communities of your students can help make for a harmonious classroom experience for teachers and students alike.
> 2. Using social media and cell phones to reach out to the families of your students in simple but frequent ways.
> 3. Communicating with students' caregivers in a way that inspires a collaborative relationship that will serve the students' best interests.
> 4. Simple ideas for being present in the community you serve.

## References

Burgess, S., & Houf, B. (2017). *Lead like a pirate: Make school amazing for your students and staff*. San Diego, CA: Dave Burgess Consulting.

Epstein, J. L. (1995). School, family, and community partnerships: Caring for the children we share. *Phi Delta Kappan, 76*(9), 701–712.

Ferlazzo, L. (2011). Involvement or engagement? *Educational Leadership, 68*(8), 10–14.

Green, S. (2013). *Race, community, and urban schools: Partnering with African American families*. New York, NY: Teachers College Press.

Hattie, J. (2009). *Visible learning: A synthesis of over 800 meta-analyses relating to achievement*. London: Routledge.

Lahey, J. (2017). *The downside of checking kids' grades constantly*. Retrieved from www.nytimes.com/2017/08/22/well/family/the-downside-of-checking-kids-grades-constantly.html

Teaching Tolerance. (2017). *Home visits*. Retrieved from www.tolerance.org/magazine/fall-2017/home-visits

# 8

# Effort and Joy, They're Not Just for Students!

> **The BIG Idea**
> *If a teacher is to cultivate a climate of joy and effort, s/he must cultivate it in her/himself as well!*
>
> **In this chapter you will:**
> 1. Learn the phases that teachers cycle through in a typical year.
> 2. Read about why a tight focus can keep a teacher happy and healthy.
> 3. Browse options for keeping yourself learning through meaningful professional development.
> 4. Reflect on your core values and how to use them to guide your decision-making.
> 5. Learn strategies for practicing self-care.

Are you overworked? Are you tired? Do you feel like you do too much? Are there times when you dread Sunday because you know it means Monday is just around the corner? Do you ever just feel burned out?

If you are a teacher who can't answer yes to at least some of these questions, you are rare indeed! Teaching is a tough job. The unique combination of social, emotional, and intellectual requirements of the profession can make it exhausting to the point of being completely overwhelming.

Yet, if you're like most of the teachers I know, you love the job, even when you feel slightly burned out. Teaching is hard. If it is to be a doable and long-lasting career, then we must do two things. One, point our efforts in the most impactful direction and, two, increase and sustain joy in our working lives.

Some years ago, as a part of a training to become a mentor for new teachers, I read Ellen Moir's theory of the phases a first-year teacher moves through (Scherer, 1999). I remember thinking that the phases seemed more universal to a teaching career than specific to that first year.

| Phase | Time of Year | Description |
| --- | --- | --- |
| Anticipation | August/September | The anticipation stage is characterized by a sense of excitement and possibility! Teachers are full of energy and raring to go! |
| Survival | October/November | In survival mode, teachers have a sense of there not being enough time, of treading water, and even of self-doubt and anxiety about their fitness for the job. |
| Disillusionment | December/January | With disillusionment, the self-doubt and anxiety intensify. Teachers can even feel a sense of dread at each coming Monday. The job seems impossible. |
| Rejuvenation | February/March | Rejuvenation happens after the winter break, and at this phase teachers show an increase in morale and some of their excitement for the work returns. |
| Reflection | April/May | During the reflection phase, teachers think about what went well (or didn't) and enthusiastically plan for the years to come. |
| Anticipation | Summer | This phase matches the first! The phases are cyclical. |

Look at the chart (above) with the phases and ask yourself if you find them to be similar to your experience each year. They sure match mine. In fact,

> **Your Turn!**
> ★ Reflect on the phases of a first-year teacher.
> ★ Ask yourself if they are familiar to you, whether you are in your first year, your tenth, or your twenty-fifth.

most veteran teachers I know recognize the phases. Whether they are experienced in a single year, several years, or over the course of an entire career, the cycle of anticipation, survival, disillusionment, rejuvenation, reflection, and anticipation is familiar to most teachers.

One possible key to longevity as an educator is to stay in those high phases (anticipation, rejuvenation, and reflection) more and linger less in those low ones (survival and disillusionment). Another key is to stay focused on what really matters and to intentionally cultivate joy in your day-to-day teaching.

## Focus On Your Efforts Where They Matter!

Teaching is a busy business. There is never enough time to do all that needs to be done. A long time ago, when I was student teaching under the guidance of the fabulous Mr. Ken Swift, I learned a valuable lesson. Ken said to me, "Teaching can be a 24/7 job. I mean, you could literally work twenty-four hours a day for seven days a week and still not be done. You have to *choose* not to."

Part of making that choice is homing in on what is really important. This topic was discussed in Chapter 4 concerning standards-focused teaching and well-honed learning targets. It was also broached in that same chapter in the discussion on quality work and why less tends to be more. Knowing your core values and relying on them to lead you down the best path is another way to stay focused on what matters most in your day-to-day life as a teacher.

### Define Your Values

Classroom teachers make something like 1,500 decisions a day (TeachThought, 2016). Take a minute to think about the types of decisions you make on any given day. Some are seemingly simple and offered as responses to student or colleague questions. You have to choose to permit or deny.

- Can I go to the bathroom?
- Can I sharpen my pencil?
- Can I finish this after lunch?

Others are more intertwined with long-term goals.

- Are the students getting it?
- What curriculum objectives can I gloss over so I can meet other, more important ones?
- How can I talk to an angry parent?

In my role as a principal, some of the decisions I make are high stakes.

- Should a student be suspended?
- How do I handle employee conflict?
- Should I push for a new strategy, rule, or initiative?
- How do I balance parent needs with teacher needs?

We make so many decisions on a daily basis that we're not always even aware that we're making them. For the most part, that's okay. But, all things being equal, being mindful of what is driving the choices we make is a good idea. A good place to start is by defining your own core values.

A simple way to do that is to look through a list of typical core values (google "core values list") and choose 10 or so that resonate with you. Then look at the values you picked and try to group them into common topics.

Next, look at the common topics and decide if you can choose one word that best defines each. Finally, whittle the grouped or single core values to the five that most closely align with your vision of your best self.

Here is an example of my work to choose the core values that best represent me.

My First List:

| love | compassion | empathy | tolerance |
|---|---|---|---|
| effort | growth | quality | equity |

My Second List (Grouped):
My Core Values:

1 Love
2 Effort
3 Optimism
4 Trust
5 Humor

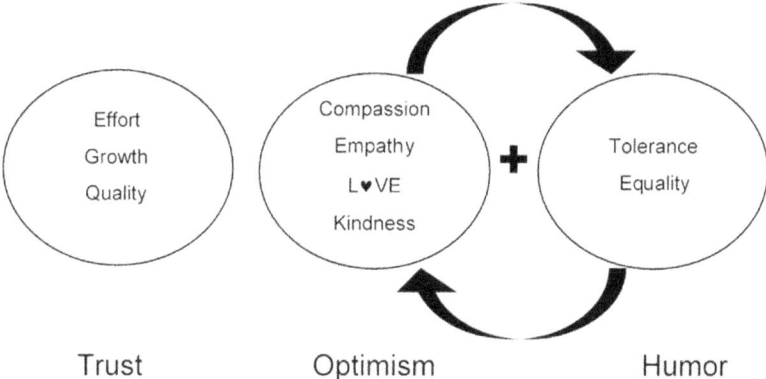

Figure 8.1 Grouping my core values.

Staying true to my core values and beliefs about how to live my best life is of paramount importance. I have learned that I feel best when I have clarity about the reasons behind my decisions. Knowing my core values helps me not only to make decisions but also, and perhaps more importantly, to determine the reasons I am making them. This clarity keeps me focused, hardworking, and, for the most part, happy.

I start and end every day by reviewing my core values, because I know that keeping them in the forefront of my thoughts will help me keep them close to my heart as well. Read the Chinese proverb below. It really describes the whats and whys of keeping core values in your thoughts and on your lips.

> *Be careful of your thoughts, for your thoughts become your words.*
> *Be careful of your words, for your words become your actions.*
> *Be careful of your actions, for your actions become your habits.*
> *Be careful of your habits, for your habits become your character.*
> *Be careful of your character, for your character becomes your destiny.*
>                                             *– Chinese proverb, author unknown*

**Your Turn!**
- ★ Use the process above to begin your journey toward finding and defining your own core values.

## Using Your Values to Make Decisions

The next step is to use your core values as a filter through which to run the decisions you make. I use the following questions to help me reflect.

1. How will the action inspired by the decision help me live out my core values?
2. Is the action really important?
3. Will it help students be more independent?
4. Will it help students be more successful?

Even if I feel I am being true to my core values, unless the answer to at least one of my questions is a firm yes, I believe that there is no reason to take action and so I don't.

Examples from the field

Below are examples of two decisions I've made that illustrate my process well.

*Example 1:* ***Quiet in the halls!***

About five years ago, my school developed our mission statement, and borrowing from Positive Behavior Intervention Supports (PBIS) practices, we made matrices to show students what it looks like to be an "independent and successful Saint who C.A.R.E.S. (cooperates, is assertive, is responsible, is empathetic, and is self-controlled)" in various areas of the school. Look below to see the matrix for behavior in the hallway.

| | |
|---|---|
| **Cooperation** | Zero volume level, walk facing forward, stay in line, watch where you are going |
| **Assertion** | Use your words when needed, ask for help when needed |
| **Responsibility** | Pay attention to staying in line, be patient while waiting |
| **Empathy** | Be respectful to other classes, say "excuse" me, smile at people you pass by |
| **Self-Control** | Keep your hands and feet to yourself, leave other people's property alone, keep your hands off of the walls |

Notice that the "cooperation" section calls for a "zero volume level" in the hallway. However, despite the fact that the staff had voted to enforce the rule, it never actually was enforced. When I became the principal, I had to grapple with this question:

*Should I require and enforce the zero noise in the hallway policy, or should I strike the rule entirely?*

To help me make the decision, I ran the problem through my questions, reflecting on how the solutions would relate to my beliefs. A summary of my thoughts is below under each question.

1. How will the action inspired by the decision help me live out my core values?
   *I think the action is important to optimism, effort, and love. I know it will be hard, but I think with some effort we can all hold each other accountable. The majority of the staff is frustrated by the few who aren't on board. We made the decision together; I owe it to the staff to enforce it. I also know that allowing students the chance to practice self-control is a gift I can give. Another reason is that when the kids are loud in halls, classes are disrupted. I think I love the students and teachers enough to watchdog this and see it through.*
2. Is the action really important?
   *Yes. It will help students practice self-control. It will decrease disruptions to classes, which are bothered by hallway noise. It will help the staff see me as a leader who can be trusted to keep my word and hold all accountable to collaborative decisions.*
3. Will it help students be more independent?
   *Not really. But it will grow their skills for being good members of society. Holding them accountable to a zero noise level in the hallway will help students practice cooperation, empathy, and especially self-control.*
4. Will it help students be more successful?
   *Ultimately, yes. Students with self-control tend to be more successful throughout their lives* (Laitsch, 2006).

After thinking it through, I decided that I should require and enforce the zero noise in the hallway policy. I have done just that, and it has gone very well! Teachers and students report that, for the most part, they appreciate the rule and my efforts to stay true to it.

*Example 2:* **What did you call me?**

When a student was wildly inappropriate on the bus, the transportation director and I decided that we had to issue him a two-day suspension from riding. That was an easy decision to make; it ran smoothly through my filtering questions. But it led to a harder choice I had to make when the father of the suspended child, who was very angry, swore at me, in the worst of ways. Though I have a really thick skin, tend to not be ego-driven, and am basically easy-going, I was taken aback. I ended the meeting but was left with a question to answer:

Should I focus on my feeling of anger and take action, confronting the father about his rude behavior, or should I let it go? When I ran this question through my values-based filter, I came to a conclusion that made me feel good.

1. How will the action inspired by the decision help me live out my core values?
   *Taking action wouldn't be in alignment with my core values. But letting it go and moving on would.*
2. Is the action really important?
   *No. Confronting the dad for swearing at me when he was really angry will do nothing to make the situation better for me, him, or his children.*
3. Will it help students be more independent?
   *No. In fact, the student doesn't even know about it.*
4. Will it help students be more successful?
   *No. In fact, if the student were to find out about it, it might damage our relationship and make it harder for him to be successful.*

In the end, I decided to let it go and rely on my core values of optimism and love, thinking that my relationship with the student's father would improve with time and empathizing with the fact that he was angry and feeling out of control. I also relied on my core value of humor, and I went home, told my husband a funny version of the story, and laughed it off.

**Continued Learning**

If we want our students to work hard, we also have to work hard. That means that staying on top of our own professional development is critical.

I often hear teachers lament that they need more training on various methods, strategies, ideas, and initiatives before they feel prepared to teach using them. While it would be wonderful for each of us to get all the training and support we need during the school day, that simply does not seem to be in the realm of any school district's hope or ability to promise.

As professionals, it is up to us to get what we need, to be self-starters and autonomous learners, much in the way most of us hope for our students to be. You're clearly interested in continued learning, or you would be watching a reality show on TV instead of reading this book! As state departments of education and local districts continue to call for "proof" of professional development in the form of renewal credits, CEUs (continuing education units), and professional learning logs, your ability to choose what and how you learn is important.

Socrates is often quoted as having said, "Education is a kindling of a flame, not the filling of a vessel." Teachers, in the 21st century, that flame is burning all over the internet. It's time to warm yourself by the cyber-fire! Call on the resources below to get the training you need.

### Graduate credit on the cheap

If you need three credits but don't want to pay university fees or find the time for face-to-face, meat-in-the-seat classes, try an online course. Most are easy to navigate and asynchronous, which means you can work on them when and where you choose. (Which for me often means at midnight in my jammies with a glass of wine at my side. If that's wrong, I don't want to be right!)

### Professional Development Institute *(PDI)*

www.webteaching.com/ and
*Learner's Edge* www.learnersedgeinc.com/courses
PDI and Learner's Edge offer very low-cost graduate credit in online environments. Both allow teachers to explore topics in education with a cost of less than $400 per three credits. If you can't find a course you like from PDI or Learner's Edge, you can build your own course with a custom study. For example, I once worked with a team of teachers who wanted to study the scholarship on engaging African American middle schools boys in reading. We chose our own text and off we went!

### MOOCs (massive online open courses)

*Coursera* www.coursera.org/ and *Edx* www.edx.org/
MOOCs are an amazing gift of the 21st century! If you have ever wanted to take a course from a master professor out of Harvard or Stanford or Yale but didn't think it was possible, you were wrong! Not only is it possible, it is *free*! Many universities are offering online courses or learning modules free of cost to teachers. They mostly consist of videos, readings, and online discussions. While credit is not always available, it certainly would count as evidence of professional development in whatever form of "teacher accountability" or "educator effectiveness" program is imposed on you. Not to mention that sometimes as professionals we need to learn not for the sake of credits or credentials but because we need to know something to make our teaching more effective. The best part about a MOOC is that you can participate in the parts you are interested in and ignore the parts that don't seem to pertain to your learning needs.

### Twitter

If you haven't yet, get yourself a handle, then use TweetDeck or HootSuite to make a free account and start tweeting in a *chat* today! A *chat* is a focused hour of tweeting with teachers all over the country on a given educational topic.

Do a search for "Twitter education chats" and you will turn up some helpful hashtag lists (chats are always done with hashtags). For example, #mschat is a regular Thursday conversation among anyone interested in middle school. If you do a web search for #mschat, you'll find all the tweets with that hashtag. Among them will likely be the time and date of the next chat. If you're not ready to tweet during a chat, just "lurk" (a somewhat creepy Twitter-term for observing a chat). Chances are you'll soon want to dive in. You can also start by following an edu-favorite. You will be amazed at the level of interaction that you can achieve with some of your edu-heroes. If you ever have a question you need answered by a leader in the field, drop them a tweet (or an email). I am continually shocked by how many respond and how quickly they do. Sometimes I wonder if these folks are sitting at their desks just waiting for someone to ask them to talk about their favorite topics! I have been able to converse with Regie Routman (@regieroutman), Dr. Mary Howard (@DrMaryHoward), Larry Ferlazzo (@Larryferlazzo), Kylene Beers (@KyleneBeers), Gail Boushey and Joan Moser (@gailandjoan), Stephen Krashen (@skrashen), and many more! While you're finding folks to follow, add me (@ritaplatt) and MiddleWeb (@MiddleWeb) as well!

### Edcamp
www.edcamp.org/
Simply put, edcamps are free conferences for teachers by teachers. Topics and sessions are generated on the spot, and attendees can present, listen, and converse in as many or as few as they would like. Although they don't happen in cyber-space, the topics are often tech-heavy. Two things are virtually guaranteed if you go: You will network and you will learn! Edcamps are sweeping the edu-world. Get out there and attend one near you.

### Google (Yes, I said, "Google!")
Honestly, the go-to place for me when I need to learn about a new topic in education is a Google search. When I wanted to learn more about Response to Intervention, PBIS, and standards-based learning (three hot topics in my district), I googled them. Of course, the internet is called "the web" for a reason, and one resource led to another and another. I saved the links that looked promising in a folder on my toolbar and read them at my leisure, and soon I felt like I had a good handle on each topic.

However you chose to learn, share the experiences with your students. When you tell them about the course you're taking or the book you're reading or the famous educator you connected with, not only can it help students

> **Your Turn!**
> 
> ★ Try cyber-learning! Start by doing one or more of the following:
>    o Sign up for a free Twitter account and follow some of the educators you respect.
>    o Go to one of the MOOC sites and find a class you're interested in.
>    o Find a graduate course that meets your unique professional development needs.
>    o Find an edcamp in your neck of the woods and then find a fellow educator to attend it with you.
>    o Choose a topic from this book (joyful learning, mastery learning, social learning, positive school climate, differentiated instruction, for example) and "google" it to see what resources you can find to further your learning.

to see you as "walking the walk" but also it can show students that learning is always a lifelong endeavor.

### Simple Tips, Hints, and Ideas for Focusing Your Efforts in the Classroom

In addition to all the ideas that were shared above, try integrating the following advice into your daily teaching life.

1. Collaborate and communicate

   Teaching was never meant to be a do-it-yourself endeavor! The internet is loaded with great lesson plans, ideas, and activities. Your colleagues are also great resources. Remember that teachers have always lived by the motto of "beg, borrow, and steal" when it comes to planning. Give it a try by opening a browser and searching Google for a topic you're about to teach. For example, "Civil War lesson plans 7th grade." You will be amazed at the results.

2. Stay in the power zone

   Where do you spend most of your class time? Behind your desk? At tables with students? On your feet, moving from spot to spot? Front and center? All of the above? It turns out that where you are in proximity to the students you are teaching can have a huge impact on their learning, their behavior, and the overall classroom climate (Cain & Laird, 2011). Think of your classroom as having three basic teaching areas:

   1. *the teacher work area (desk or computer table)*
   2. *the lecture position (at the front of the class)*
   3. *the "power zone" (right in the middle of all of the action!)*

It's probably abundantly clear that the best place to teach is named the power zone! While there will always be times when the most appropriate place to teach from is either the front of the room or your desk, the vast majority of teaching time should be spent sitting with or moving among and between your students. To this end, many of the teachers in my school are moving away from having teacher's desks at all, and that is probably a good thing: you can't sit behind a desk you don't have!

3  One sentence lesson plans

Dr. Norman Eng (2017) is a teacher who, like many of us, had let formal lesson plans slip to the wayside. As he puts it, "Who's got time to write *full* lesson plans? For every class? Five days a week? There's no way to know what'll happen Friday when so much changes on Monday" (Eng, 2017). But he is acutely aware of how important it is to know the whats, hows, and whys of the lessons we teach, so he developed what he calls the *one sentence lesson plan*.

If you think back (or look back) at Chapter 2, you will remember the three important questions that you want students to be able to answer if they are to fully engage with the content you are teaching. Those questions are:

1   *What am I learning?*
2   *Why am I learning it?*
3   *How will I know when I've learned it?*

But if you don't know the answers to those questions well in advance of teaching a lesson, how can your students? Think of the one sentence lesson plan as answering these similar questions:

1   *What am I teaching?*
2   *Why am I teaching it?*
3   *What method(s) will I use?*
4   *How will I know when students have learned it?*

Now, I'll be honest, I have never been able to get the plan into one neat sentence, but truly the function is more important than the form. As I often remind the teachers at my school, "These are basic questions that we should be able to answer anytime anyone asks." These questions help keep us on track, focused, and working hard to help our students master content. Look at the example below for more clarity. Note, it is not one sentence, but it is way more succinct than a formal lesson plan would be!

*I am teaching students to use varied sentence lengths in their writing because I have noticed most of them are using very short sentences, and strong sentence fluency is one of the traits good writers use. I will read students an example and have them highlight short and long sentences in a text, and we will do a shared writing. I will know they "get it" when their writing is comprised of sentences with a mix of lengths.*

4 Purge!

If you haven't used it in three years, chances are you're not going to use it again. Pitch it! Clutter is a breeding ground for stress, and stress robs teachers of precious time and energy that could be better focused. Turn on the tunes and spend a day sorting, organizing, recycling, and even throwing away. This is especially important for teachers who have been in the same classroom for several years. This year, a teacher at my school, Mrs. Sladky, spent an entire week purging. I spent one day helping her, and as we boxed up and donated supplies, books, and lesson plans she hadn't used in years, I could almost see the stress melt away. When we were all finished, she said, "I should have done this years ago." Don't wait! Get your purge on now!

5 Divide your to-do list

Teachers' to-do lists can seem endless. To manage them, prioritize by dividing them into the categories below.

- *Today* – things that *must* be done ASAP, including meetings, phone calls to parents, following through on job-related due dates, etc.
- *This Week* – things that are a priority but can wait if needed. For example, writing next week's lesson plans, getting ready for events that will occur in the near future, entering grades, or writing the classroom newsletter.
- *This Month* – things that need to be done in a timely but not an urgent manner. Such as updating the class webpage, making a new seating chart, changing a bulletin board, finalizing grades, and getting ready for parent-teacher conferences.
- *Someday/Maybe* – things that you would like to do but that don't make or break your classroom. For example, redesigning your classroom storage or webpage, redesigning your curriculum, writing an article, etc.

---

**Your Turn!**

★ Monitor your teaching and identify how often you are in the power zone. Make a plan to get there more often!

★ Write a one (or more) sentence lesson plan for something you plan to teach soon.

★ Develop a divided to-do list and celebrate each time you cross an item off!

## Staying Joyful!

The thesis of this book is that the most successful classrooms are those with cultures that inspire students to be both hardworking and happy. Above, ideas were shared to help teachers stay focused and hone their efforts such that they are the best they can be for their students. But equally important is that teachers are happy. Below are strategies that just might help teachers stay joyful.

### Start and End With Love

No matter what is happening, try to focus on love. I know that makes me sound hippy-dippy. But when we remind ourselves that we are the stewards of our fellow human beings, it becomes easier to accept the behaviors they display, and we can encourage ourselves to stay positive.

This is especially true if you have students who have difficult behaviors. Focusing on love (for teaching and for students) helps you remember to dislike the behavior but not the person. When you start from a place of love, it is pretty difficult to end up at a place of anger or other negative emotions.

### Stop the Ripples of Rudeness

It is hard to feel joyful when people are rude. But, let's face it, sometimes our fellow teachers are. Think of a time someone was rude to you at school. Maybe they took the last cup of coffee or left the copy machine jammed. Or maybe when you walked into another teacher's room, he didn't look up and greet you, or someone took the space where you always park. How did it make you feel? What did you do with that feeling?

The research on how being treated rudely affects people who encounter it is fascinating. Experiencing rude behaviors can have deep and lasting impacts. Even witnessing rude behavior that is not personally directed is harmful (Woolum, Foulk, Lanaj, & Erez, 2017). Sarah DiGiulio (2018) summarizes the effects, saying rude interactions tend to ripple out and have lasting negative impacts. She writes, "We tend to ruminate about rude interactions – maybe talking about it with our friends, thinking about it later in the day, or letting it wake us up in the middle of the night."

DiGiulio points out that that even when behaviors seem minor, they may not be innocuous and that rudeness "instigates a self-perpetuating cycle of negative behavior, hampering our productivity, our happiness and our health along the way."

Below is advice for culling rude behavior or learning to let it go so that it doesn't impact your ability to be joyful.

1. *Acknowledge people and express appreciation*. The simple act of spreading appreciation can counteract rudeness in lasting ways. If you

think something nice about someone, *tell her/him*! Take the time to share kind words.

2. *Don't let rude behavior fester*. Talk to people when you are bothered. Teachers tend to follow the advice my mother always gave, "Suck it up, Buttercup!" While there is something to be said for letting rude behavior roll off your back, there is also something to be said for clearing the air. Don't hold on to anger and let it morph into resentment. If someone is rude, confront her/him with care. The key is to not let your emotions or ego rule your response. Wait until you're calm and then try saying in a calm, kind tone, "You may not have meant to be rude but when you _____, it made me feel _____. Can we talk about it?"

3. *Think about how your actions might sit with others*. People perceive things differently. This can be even more true in cross-cultural relationships. Learn about the people you spend time with and watch how they respond to you. Then, if you do offend or feel you might have, apologize. No need to make a huge deal out of it, but say you're sorry if you've been rude or even if someone thinks you were rude and you weren't. Try something like this, "I'm so sorry you felt I was rude. I didn't mean to hurt you." You're not apologizing for actually being rude, but rather saying you're sorry that someone felt you were. That's just common kind behavior.

4. *Assume best intentions*. See folks' better angels. Above, I made the extremely obvious point that people perceive things differently. Sometimes I think someone is being rude and later realize that it was not at all their intention. For five years I facilitated a professional learning community, and one of our stated norms was "Assume best intentions!" It helped remind us to not jump to negative conclusions but rather to positive ones. It made a difference in how we operated.

5. *Avoid rude people like the plague*. Even though I am a smiley-faced, rose-colored glasses wearing Pollyanna, I get that sometimes no matter how hard we try, we're going to bump up against folks who are habitually and even intentionally rude. In those cases, the best likely course of action it to avoid them as much as possible. Then, when it's impossible and you have to spend time together, I urge you to do as I tell my kids to do, "Find the funny!" Think of that rude person as a character in a sitcom. You know an Archie Bunker (*All in the Family*) or Dr. Cox (*Scrubs*) or literally anyone on *It's Always Sunny in Philadelphia* and *Seinfeld*. Those rude/mean characters are funny! See if you can giggle a little to melt away the sting of rude folks (not at them, of course! But, maybe later when you go home and vent with your spouse or another friend).

## Practice Self-care

These days, as a teacher, you've probably already read something about "self-care." There is a movement in educircles around the more than worthy notion that teachers need to be mindful of meeting their own needs. You know, the "put on your oxygen mask first" theory of supporting kids. It's a good theory.

Teachers work hard and often do so with little regard for their own needs. That's not sustainable. If we want to serve our students, then truly we must be reasonably healthy and happy ourselves. That means we've got to engage in some self-care.

When I did (an admittedly quick) Google search, I found a common list of self-care strategies.

- Meditate
- Exercise
- Sleep more
- Work less
- Take up a hobby

I truly believe self-care is important, but I don't want to take breaks, do yoga, or take a brisk walk around the building, and I certainly don't want to eat less on my school's famous "Chip Thursday" shared snack days. So while there is nothing wrong with these common tips for helping teachers stay emotionally healthy, they just don't fit all of us. I am happiest and feel healthiest when I am busy, and I suspect there are others out there who, like me, look for a less quiet, introspective kind of self-care.

One great way to recharge is to get a daily dose of gut-busting laughter. Believe it or not, laughing as self-care is a scientifically proven strategy that works! According to the Mayo Clinic (2016), laughter is a great stress reliever. Additionally, laughing stimulates our organs, relieves pain, improves mood, deepens our sense of satisfaction with life, and even boosts our immunity (and every teacher who has worked even one day knows how germy schools are!). Mental Floss (2018) offers other benefits of laughter that fit the self-care bill, saying that when we laugh we reduce anxiety, build stronger social connections, and lower blood pressure! Below are my suggestions to help you laugh your way to balance.

The internet is a fertile ground for those who need a good laugh. Check out any of the education-related video series below when you need one.

- *Principal Gerry Brooks* (www.gerrybrooksprin.com/): Principal Brooks makes short funny videos about life as an educator that are

often laugh-out-loud funny. Try his behavior management videos; they are as instructive as they are hilarious.
- *Kid Snippets* (www.youtube.com/user/BoredShortsTV): Kid Snippets are videos that feature the conversations of kids reenacted by adults. Math Class is my favorite, and it seems that no matter how many times I watch it, I laugh hard.
- *Key & Peele* (www.cc.com/shows/key-and-peele): Keegan-Michael Key and Jordan Peele are a sketch comedy duo who have done several bits on teaching and learning. If you still haven't seen the Substitute Teacher, Part 1, you must!

If you prefer reading, try any of the blogs or books below. I promise you won't be disappointed!

- Literally any joke book! Honestly! Get a joke book at the thrift store or bookmark a website with jokes. Then read one or two of them each day. Even better, ask a student to tell you a joke. Kid jokes are often so bad that they become funny by default.
- *Adequate Yearly Progress* by Roxanna Elden: This novel is set in an urban high school that has been deemed failing. The teachers and the students deal with the daily struggles of teaching and learning under the watchful eyes of carpetbagger consultants and corrupt leaders. The themes are dark to be sure, but that doesn't stop Elden from delivering big laughs.
- *32 Third Graders and One Classroom Bunny* by Phillip Donne: This one is written by a third grade teacher (obviously) and offers short but super funny anecdotes about his days in the classroom. Even though the teacher is sharing elementary-age funnies, teachers of any grade will recognize the scenarios he shares.
- Books by comedians: Honestly, I love so many of these that I couldn't pick just one. Below are some of my favorites from the last couple of years. For a real treat, get an audible version and listen to them while you do chores. Most are so funny that I actually like cleaning the house and doing the laundry if I can listen while doing it! As an added bonus, many of the books listed below are also memoirs or autobiographies. That means you get to learn about a life that might be very different from your own while you laugh.
  - *Dad Is Fat* by Jim Gaffigan
  - *Hi Bob!* by Bob Newhart
  - *A Polaroid Guy in a Snapchat World* by David Spade (Warning! This is not for the easily offended! There is a good amount of raunchy humor here.)

- – *The Last Black Unicorn* by Tiffany Haddish
  - – *I Can't Make This Up: Life Lessons* by Kevin Hart
  - – *Furiously Happy* by Jenny Lawson
- ◆ *Love, Teach* blog (www.loveteachblog.com/): Love, Teach is an anonymous junior high teacher-blogger who is equal parts warrior for school equity issues and bumbling every-teacher storyteller. She is honest, heart-warming, and *super funny*!
- ◆ *The Tattooed Teacher* blog (https://tattooteacher.wordpress.com/): In this blog, you'll find another good dose of self-effacing humor from a sixth grade teacher, mixed in with the small everyday tales of triumph that help us all stay focused on moving forward.

**Simple Tips, Hints, and Ideas to Keep You Joyful in the Classroom**
Sometimes it's the little things that help us to stay joyful. Below are four great ways to get and stay happy.

1  Learn to say "No"!
   We teachers are giving by nature. But to remain at the top of our game, we have to learn to say no. Limit yourself to one or two committees at a time. Don't commit to more than one or two school activities per quarter. Only go to the meetings you must attend. Learn to trust others to pick up the slack. Being over-committed and exhausted will not do you or your students any good.

2  Don't obsess
   Obsession is the dark side of reflection. Be reflective, not obsessive. Being a reflective teacher means constantly examining your efforts and their results with a goal toward improving future learning. There are, however, some aspects of the job that you shouldn't spend much time thinking about. These include job requirements that you have no control over, personal interactions that are history, and mistakes that you can move on from.
   School reform expert Michael Fullan (2010) reminds us that teaching is a "ready-fire-aim" enterprise. It's a complex job and you're bound to make mistakes. Learn from them but don't obsess over them. You don't have the time or the energy for that.

3  Recognize that great can be the enemy of good enough
   Be kind to yourself. You do not have to be perfect. In fact, modeling the way you handle mistakes is good for students. Learn to be happy with papers, projects, and assignments that are a shade or two less than

perfect. You have a growth-mindset for your students. Offer yourself that same gift.

An astonishing number of teachers leave the field due to burnout. Don't be one of them. None of the tips above is revolutionary, and none will make your job a nine-to-five. But they might help a little. A little bit of time saved, a little bit of help gained, might be the difference between being in that sweet spot and being in the survival zone.

4  Get out there and have fun!

If possible, find a like-minded group of teachers to socialize with. Establishing a weekly, monthly, or even just quarterly social hour can help teachers connect, support one and other, laugh together, and generally breed happiness at work.

I recommend spending some social time with other teachers as a part of your self-care regimen. Meet in the "faculty lounge" (AKA Applebees or *gasp* the local tavern) for "book club," a "staff meeting," or a "PLC" committee meeting (note the quotes). Eat together, drink together, be merry together! The bottom line is that happy teachers lead happy classrooms. We owe it to ourselves and to our students to have some fun! That counts as self-care, too!

> **Recapping the BIG Idea**
>
> *If a teacher is to cultivate a climate of joy and effort, s/he must cultivate it in her/himself as well!*
>
> **In this chapter we looked at:**
> 1. The phases that teachers cycle through in a typical year.
> 2. Options for keeping yourself learning through meaningful professional development.
> 3. Reflecting on your core values and how to use them to guide your decision-making.
> 4. Practicing self-care.

## References

Cain, S., & Laird, M. (2011). *The fundamental 5: The formula for quality instruction*. Place of publication not identified: Publisher not identified.

DiGiulio, S. (2018). *Psychologists say rudeness is a habit you should ditch – stat*. Retrieved from www.nbcnews.com/better/pop-culture/why-rudeness-so-toxic-how-stop-it-ncna876131

Done, P. (2009). 32 third graders and one class bunny: Life lessons from teaching. New York: Simon & Schuster.

Elden, R. (2018). *Adequate yearly progress: A novel*. Rivet Street Books.

Eng, N. (2017). *Introducing the one-sentence lesson plan*. Retrieved from www.cultofpedagogy.com/one-sentence-lesson-plan/

Fullan, M. (2010). *Motion leadership: The skinny on becoming change savvy*. Thousand Oaks, CA: Corwin.

Gaffigan, J. (2013). Dad is fat. New York: Three Rivers Press.

Haddish, T. (2019). The last black unicorn. New York: Gallery Books.

Hart, K. (2016). I can't make this up: life lessons. New York: Simon & Scheuster.

Laitsch, D. (2006). *Self-discipline and student academic achievement*. Retrieved from www.ascd.org/publications/researchbrief/v4n06/toc.aspx

Lawson, J. (2017). Furiously happy: A funny book about horrible things. New York, NY: Flatiron Books.

Mayo Clinic. (2016). *Stress relief from laughter? It's no joke*. Retrieved from www.mayoclinic.org/healthy-lifestyle/stress-management/in-depth/stress-relief/art-20044456

Newhart, B. (2018). Hi Bob! Audible Originals, LLC.

Rosenfeld, J. (2018). *11 scientific benefits of having a laugh*. Retrieved from http://mentalfloss.com/article/539632/scientific-benefits-having-laugh

Scherer, M. (1999). *A better beginning supporting and mentoring new teachers*. Alexandria, VA: Association for Supervision and Curriculum Development.

Spade, D. (2018). A polaroid guy in a snapchat world. Audible Originals, LLC.

TeachThought. (2016). *A teacher makes 1500 educational decisions a day*. Retrieved from www.teachthought.com/pedagogy/teacher-makes-1500-decisions-a-day/

Woolum, A., Foulk, T., Lanaj, K., & Erez, A. (2017). Rude color glasses: The contaminating effects of witnessed morning rudeness on perceptions and behaviors throughout the workday. *Journal of Applied Psychology, 102*(12), 1658–1672.

# 9

# Conclusion

## Create a Brand New BHAG

The best classrooms are those where effort and joy, hard work, and happy fun are woven together in tight braids of learning. Every student deserves a teacher who will insist that s/he can learn, will learn, and will be held accountable to excellence. Every student deserves a teacher who will cultivate a joyful, safe, and happy learning space. I want to be that teacher. As a principal, I want all of the teachers at my school to be that teacher.

## Remember the BIG Idea

The title of this book, *Working Hard, Working Happy*, is the big idea in a nutshell. When we engineer our classrooms or schools such that students expect to apply effort and work hard in a joyful environment, then we create climates that are conducive to maximum learning.

> **Effort + Joy = Learning**

## The Five-part Philosophy

I want to end this book in much the same way I began it. In Chapter 1, I shared my five-part philosophy that might also be called my top five list of the best practices in teaching. As I explained, I began the process of defining my beliefs many years ago, when, at the very beginning of my career, a professor asked me to identify my philosophy of education. It didn't come easy. After reading about the ideas of Dewey, Freire, Bloom, Montessori, Hirsch, and Bagley, I was able to develop a nascent philosophy statement about students being active participants who sought to learn and looked to their teachers to guide them.

What continues to surprise and delight me is that, for the most part, I have stayed true to that early glimmer of a philosophy, just as the professor had told me I would. Perhaps even more important, my philosophy of teaching and learning, now in five parts, permeates all I do. I hope that as you revisit the five big beliefs that drive my work as an educator; you'll find that they resonated strongly throughout the contents of this book. And I hope that you'll be inspired to draft a teaching philosophy of your own, if you haven't started already!

1. Every single student can grow, learn, and achieve at high levels. All students should be offered a rigorous curriculum that focuses on growth.
2. Joy is critical for learning. When students are joyful, they will take more risks, meet more challenges, and generally learn better.
3. The best teachers are coaches, not facilitators or bosses.
4. Motivation is key, but the way we think of motivation must change.
5. Classroom management is absolutely foundational to teaching and learning.

Having a classroom/school where all students work hard, feel supported, and see themselves as joyful is my BHAG! BHAG is an acronym for "Big Hairy Audacious Goal" (Buchanan, 2012). As Buchanan says, "The power of the BHAG is that it gets you out of thinking too small. A great BHAG changes the time frame and simultaneously creates a sense of urgency."

I realize that this is a huge goal. I realize that from year to year our classes change and so does the mood of the class. I have had tough classes. While I am an optimist to the extreme, I am also a realist. I know that I can't make every student see the value of hard work or insist that they are all happy in my care. But I can try. I hope you will try too!

## Okay. Joy & Effort. Now What?

So, what's next? Reflect. Decide on your own BHAG. Make goals to get there. But don't be in a huge hurry. One step at a time is fine. Be kind to yourself and move forward at a sustainable pace. Feel free to use the questions below

> **Your Turn!**
> - What is your BHAG?
> - What is your philosophy of education?
> - How do you cultivate joy in your classroom?
> - How do you differentiate learning opportunities such that each student can work hard and as a result can demonstrate mastery through quality work?
> - Do you have strong relationships with your students, their caregivers, and others in the learning community? How can you strengthen them?
> - Do you use the power of social connections and social proof to motivate students to work hard and be joyful in your classroom?
> - Are you helping students take ownership of their learning by teaching them to set, monitor, and meet their own goals?
> - Are you taking care of your own needs before trying to meet the needs of others?

to get you started or feel free to ignore them completely and let practices that cultivate joy and effort seep into your practices more organically. Either way, thank you for reading this book and best wishes for a classroom filled with happy and hardworking students.

## Reference

Buchanan, L. (2012). *Jim Collins: How to achieve big, hairy, audacious goals*. Retrieved from www.inc.com/leigh-buchanan/big-ideas/jim-collins-big-hairy-audacious-goals.html

For Product Safety Concerns and Information please contact our EU representative GPSR@taylorandfrancis.com
Taylor & Francis Verlag GmbH, Kaufingerstraße 24, 80331 München, Germany

www.ingramcontent.com/pod-product-compliance
Lightning Source LLC
Chambersburg PA
CBHW080938300426
44115CB00017B/2871